Iain Wightwick is a barrister at Unity Street Chambers in Bristol. He is a specialist property lawyer and has a particular interest in social housing, with a focus on neighbour nuisance and related anti-social behaviour matters ('neighbours from hell'), housing disrepair and homelessness. As part of his caseload, he is often instructed to pursue claims for ASBIs and for ASB-related possession and is occasionally briefed on behalf of defendants. Many of the disputes include consideration of issues relating to disabilities and the Equality Act 2010. He has thirty years' experience of acting for social landlords and tenants, and a reputation for creative, cost-controlling approaches to litigation and to alternative dispute resolution.

A Practical Guide to Antisocial Behaviour Injunctions

Second Edition

A Practical Guide to Antisocial Behaviour Injunctions

Second Edition

Iain Wightwick, BSc. Hons, Dip. Law

Barrister, Unity Street Chambers, Bristol

Law Brief Publishing

Published 2023 by Law Brief Publishing, an imprint of Law Brief Publishing Ltd
30 The Parks
Minehead
Somerset
TA24 8BT

www.lawbriefpublishing.com

Paperback: 978-1-914608-95-7

This book is dedicated to my long-suffering wife, known to many as 'St. Anne', for her unending patience with my own antisocial behaviour, and to my family and friends, who make it all worthwhile.

PREFACE

Although the pursuit of an application for an antisocial behaviour injunction ("ASBI") might appear straightforward, complications can derail even the experienced practitioner. As remedies for nuisance have developed, so have the challenges of collecting evidence and of complying with procedural requirements increased.

Many issues have been resolved in appeals, but there are still areas of uncertainty for which there is no authority. Reliance on judgement and experience is necessary. The forthcoming Pre-Action Protocol ("PAP") will add to the questions to be considered by practitioners handling ASBIs.

Some of the content of this book is based on principles from cases which have come before the courts while other material is untested by the appellate courts but has worked in practice for me.

I hope that this guide helps you to navigate ASBI claims, whether you are pursuing or defending them. Please feel free to correct me if you find legal or other errors, or if you disagree with my practical suggestions.

The law is up to date as of 31st December 2022.

Iain Wightwick
January 2023

CONTENTS

TABLE OF CASES

TABLE OF LEGISLATION

INTRODUCTION
WHY STATUTORY HELP IS NECESSARY TO CONTROL ANTISOCIAL BEHAVIOUR

KEY POINTS

1. The law before 1996 left victims largely unprotected against antisocial behaviour and citizens had to put up with it, unless crimes were being committed against them.

2. Since then, the law has improved protection for the public and it is now possible to prevent many types of undesirable conduct, mostly by use of the Anti-social Behaviour, Crime and Policing Act 2014 ("the 2014 Act").

3. The 2014 Act amalgamated various earlier remedies and created new mechanisms to control behaviour.

4. The provisions relating to injunctions are probably the most complex, because there is such an interplay between the Act and the law, both substantive and procedural.

5. The ambit of ASBIs includes 'access injunctions' for gas and other safety related tenancy management issues.

6. The Civil Justice Council's Report on antisocial behaviour and the courts has recommended some changes to the current provisions, to ensure that defendants' individual characteristics are taken into account.

Before the Housing Act 1996 ("the 1996 Act") victims of anti-social behaviour could do little to protect themselves other than rely on the criminal law. The Court of Appeal was clear that the civil courts could not be used to control behaviour which did not amount to a breach of an existing legal or equitable right. The House of Lords had already found that a local council could not sue for interference with public rights unless it had suffered some special damage of its own.[1] Attempts at using the civil courts to help out the criminal courts had also met with disapproval.[2]

The 1996 Act gave victims in some housing much better chances of being able to stop nuisance perpetrators, provided their landlord was willing to help them. The remedies available were piecemeal and did not cover every situation. Further help came for victims in the form of the Crime and Disorder Act 1998 ("the 1998 Act"), which created the "ASBO". The government then obliged local authorities to formulate and implement strategies for the reduction of crime and disorder and to exercise their functions with due regard to the likely effect of the exercise of those functions on illegal/nuisance behaviour. They had to prepare a "community strategy" to promote well-being in their area.[3]

Despite this legislation, people in privately owned housing were powerless to protect themselves unless they could persuade the local authority to obtain an ASBO. Nor was there any specific protection against the activities of gang members. Attempts at using section 222 of the Local Government Act 1972 to bring a claim seeking injunctive relief in the County Court were crushed by the Court of Appeal in *Birmingham v Shafi).*[4] That decision provoked swift action from the government. In

---

1 *Stoke on Trent City Council v B&Q Retail Ltd* [1984] 1 AC 754 per Lord Templeman at pages 770-771

2 *Gouriet v Union of Post Office Workers* [1978] AC 435

3 sections 6(1) and 17 of the Crime and Disorder Act 1998 and section 4 of the Local Government Act 2000

4 *Birmingham CC v Shafi* [2008] EWCA Civ 1186. See also *Leeds City Council v* [2015] QBD in which a County Court judge said that the 2014 Act should be used to restrain antisocial behaviour, rather than section 222

2009 the police and local authorities were given the power to obtain "gang injunctions" using the Policing and Crime Act 2009. That Act also created the "Closure Order". Over the years other protection was provided against anti-social behaviour and nuisance by various other stand-alone measures.

The government then indulged in extensive consultation and research with interested parties.[5] The outcome was the drafting of the 2014 Act. The new Act applies to both public and private sector housing and provides a variety of remedies which now address activities causing a nuisance and annoyance in almost any circumstances. There are various new tools to control ASB at the disposal of the authorities.

The government wanted greater focus on the impact of anti-social behaviour on victims and on remedies for them, and also wanted to stress the importance that the legal threshold was met before the powers we used. It wanted to target remedies on specific behaviour and to ensure that there was local consultation, accountability and transparency.

The emphasis is on proportionality of the response to specific behaviour which is causing harm or nuisance, without adversely interfering with behaviour which cannot be described as unlawful or antisocial.

Gas injunctions: The ambit of ASB injunctions has been extended to include a failure by a tenant or occupant of a property to provide access, where that failure results in one of the mischiefs targeted by the Act (see Chapters One and Two). Now, landlords are able to apply under the Act for an ASBI, with a power of arrest if necessary, when a tenant's refusal of access satisfies the threshold test.

Much was made of the "Community Trigger", which can be used by victims to force authorities to review what they are doing to protect them. There is also a little-used "Community Remedy", which gives victims a

---

5 see the collection of statistics and reports on ASB prepared between 2009 and 2013, though it is only update to 2013

say in punishments where the perpetrator is dealt with through a "community resolution disposal".

The current powers are nearly sufficient, though there are a few issues with them. There have been few cries that they fail to protect the interests of the perpetrator, but in July 2020 the Civil Justice Council published a 150-page report on ASBIs. That report found that there are concerns to be addressed.

The full report can be downloaded from the Court and Tribunal's Judiciary website at www.judiciary.uk/guidance-and-resources/anti-social-behaviour-and-the-civil-courts.

It found that the Home Office and HMCTS should be asked to collect data on ASBI cases, that the NHS Liaison & Diversion Service should be widened and improved, that the scope and provision of legal aid should be widened to ensure that nobody goes to jail without access to legal advice and that a new sentencing guideline should be adopted.

Further, they concluded that a Pre-Action Protocol ("PAP") was needed, that the court should ensure adequate information is available to participants, and that the use of positive requirements needed improvement. There were other issues which it considered beyond its remit.

The PAP is discussed in Chapters One and Five, as it will become part of getting over the start line, given that defendants will ask the court to take any failures to comply into account when considering whether to make an order and the terms of that order. Breach of the Protocol might also sound in costs, creating further difficulties for applicants, particularly as costs orders can rarely be enforced against defendants. They may, e.g., be publicly funded or impecunious, Obtaining injunctions in the future is likely to become more expensive and time-consuming.

The Court of Appeal has recently (in December 2022) given judgment on three ASBI sentencing appeals, in which they commented on the CJC

Report and provided useful guidance on sentencing.[6]

6 *Christopher Lovett v Wigan Borough Council* (with two other cases) [2022] EWCA Civ 1631

CHAPTER ONE
'PASSING GO' – THE BASICS, GAS INJUNCTIONS AND THE NEW PROTOCOL

KEY POINTS

1. The Anti-social Behaviour 'threshold test'
2. Gas Injunctions
3. Housing related v non-housing cases
4. Permitting or allowing is enough
5. Other remedies if the behaviour doesn't pass the threshold test
6. Failure of alternative remedies
7. Complying with the Pre-Action Protocol

Anti-social Behaviour 'threshold test' and the PAP

1. When the various alternatives to court action are either unsuitable because of the seriousness of the problem, or they have failed to stop it, the civil injunction under Part 1 of the 2014 Act is available to control ASB as defined in section 2 of the 2014 Act.

2. The institution of a Pre-Action Protocol for ASBIs will provide a structured framework to ensure that applicants have considered how best to prevent or reduce ASB. Any competent authority will

already have had an ASB policy in force, which will have required that they should consider alternatives to an application for an injunction.

3. Given the costs in both time and legal fees, in my experience such applications are not made lightly, or when there are less expensive or more efficacious alternatives available. So perhaps the PAP will not make much difference to applicants who already have an efficient pre-application process.

4. The applicant must satisfy a clearly worded statutory test:[7] it must show the court (1) that it is a body entitled to apply for such an order, (2) on the balance of probabilities that a person aged 10 or over (3) "*has engaged in, or is threatening to engage in, anti-social behaviour*" and, (4) if so, as a matter of judgement, *"that it is just and convenient to grant the injunction*" for the purpose of preventing antisocial behaviour.

5. There is no point in thinking about applying for an injunction unless you can obtain evidence of conduct which will satisfy that test later, when the court looks carefully at the allegations, at the return date or trial. In addition, when the PAP comes into force, it will be necessary to adduce evidence of the satisfaction of its requirements before the application is made.

6. So before issuing the application, it is necessary to consider whether, when examined critically by a defendant, there is evidence of "anti-social behaviour" which can be proved to the civil standard, "on the balance of probabilities", before instituting the steps in the PAP and then applying for the injunction.

7 section 1 of the Act

Access injunctions in social housing

7. Last August, His Honour Judge Michael Berkley, sitting in the County Court at Winchester, on appeal from Swindon, gave judgment on 21 August 2021 on an application by Swindon for an ASBI against a tenant who was refusing access for the purposes of a gas safety inspection. He found for the Council. His decision is discussed in Chapter Two on satisfying the threshold tests.

8. His decision means that social landlords can now use the Act to apply for an injunction, and inappropriate circumstances can ask for a power of arrest when a tenant refuses access for a gas or other safety inspection. There is no reason why this principle should not apply in other cases where public authorities seek access for the purposes of safeguarding the public against matters which are likely to cause harassment, alarm or distress.

Housing v non-housing related cases

9. There is a significant difference between remedies available in housing related situations and those available more generally. The definition in section 2 of the 2014 Act is different depending on whether the conduct is "housing related" or not. The difference between the two needs to be considered carefully and chapter 3 is devoted to that distinction.

10. The defendant does not have to indulge in the behaviour themselves-they merely have to be shown to have allowed or permitted it to happen. The Explanatory Notes to the 2014 Act say: "*Both definitions are capable of including allowing, inciting or encouraging any other person to engage or threaten to engage in anti-social behaviour.*" Allowing includes omitting to take steps which could have been taken to prevent the conduct complained of.[8]

---

8 *Kensington and Chelsea RLBC v Simmonds* [1996] 29 H.L.R. 507 and *West Kent HA v Davies* (1998) 31 H.L.R. 415.

11. Note that 'allowing' can include letting children in one's care all partners behave antisocially. This is obviously a relevant consideration where children are behaving in an antisocial manner and the parents are not looking after them because they are leaving them home alone, or unable through the intake of drink or drugs to control their behaviour properly.

12. There are plenty of examples of where an adult defendant has not caused nuisance or annoyance themselves, yet an injunction has been made against them (and they have subsequently lost their tenancy) because they have failed adequately to ensure people living with them and visiting them do not misbehave. There will usually be a history of poor behaviour, with attempts by the authorities to improve parenting or adherence to tenancy conditions before it gets bad enough to warrant an injunction and possession proceedings.

Other remedies if the behaviour doesn't pass the threshold test

13. If the behaviour does not satisfy the test in the 2014 Act, other remedies may be available, such as mediation, community resolutions, conditional cautions and ABCs, which are outside the scope of this book. When the PAP comes into force, it will be necessary to include evidence of attempts made to avoid the need to apply for an injunction. This is addressed below and in Chapter Four when discussing the collection of evidence.

Failure of alternative remedies

14. If the conduct continues despite attempting other remedies, it may well be that what was previously insufficient can be seen as part of a course of conduct and will be enough to support an application for an injunction.

15. For instance, something which might not be a nuisance or annoyance can become so if repeated. Additionally, someone can

be accused of harassment if there are two incidents where only one would not suffice.

16. But a defendant is not entitled to say that, where an applicant has a choice between another remedy and an injunction, it should not be granted the injunction. That argument was rejected by HHJ McKenna (s/a Deputy High Court Judge) in *Birmingham City Council v Sharif,*[9] although it is not uncommon to see it in a defendant's skeleton argument.

The Statutory Guidance

17. The new statutory guidance (published June 2022) attempts to increase the use of the Community Trigger process, which allows victims to ask for a formal review of decisions taken in respect of the control of antisocial behaviour. The relevant bodies must publish every 12 months information covering the number of applications for the Community Trigger, along with other statistics including the number of case reviews that resulted in recommendations being made.

18. The guidance calls for an increased awareness of the Community Remedy when dealing with the causes of antisocial behaviour. It gives an example of requiring perpetrators to clean up graffiti or other damage, either their own or others. Many would no doubt see this as an attractive outcome in an ASB complaint.

19. Restorative Justice has also been given a heightened emphasis.

---

[9] [2019] EWHC 1268 (QB). See also. See also *Redpath v Swindon BC* [2009] EWCA Civ 943 [2010] PTSR 904, *Birmingham CC v James* [2013] EWCA Civ 552 [22], [28], [31] and *Birmingham CC v Afsar (No 3)* [2019] EWHC 3217 (QB).

Complying with the Pre-Action Protocol

20. At the time of writing in November 2022, the wording of the PAP has yet to be finalised. However, I am told that it will not be significantly different to the draft prepared by the Working Party.

Scope and Aims of the Protocol-Part 1

21. It will apply to standalone injunction applications but not where another protocol applies (e.g. possession).

22. It is intended to be consistent, and to be read in conjunction with the "Statutory Guidance for Frontline Professionals", which was updated in June 2022. Applicants also need to comply with their own internal policies, which they should provide to the court if necessary and with any local plan in relation to consultation before starting ASB proceedings.

23. The aims of the PAP are expressed in Part 1 to be:

- to encourage more pre-action contact and exchange of information between applicants and other parties (note this includes between, e.g., applicants and the police);
- to avoid litigation by agreeing "a way forward" if possible;
- to allow court time to be used more effectively if proceedings are necessary.

Balancing the interests of perpetrators and victims

24. Paragraph 1.4 recognises that a claimant's wider responsibilities "may, on occasion, limit the scope for pre-action contact and settlement", i.e. that it is not always possible to attempt to avoid litigation. In appropriate cases an ex-parte order can be sought without informing the defendant or any agencies which might otherwise be consulted, and the Protocol will not apply.

25. Part 1 continues with a statement that applications made under the 2014 Act are not like normal civil claims involving private rights, because they are brought by applicants pursuing wider public protection functions.

26. This is important to bear in mind, because even if an application is not successful, it should not follow that any criticism can or should be made of the applicant. This might mean, for instance, that no adverse order for costs might be made if the application is dismissed, particularly for some technical reason. In general, the courts will be reluctant to impose costs orders against bodies pursuing such public protection functions in any event.

Considering the particular characteristics of the respondent

27. Paragraph 1.7 of Part 1 requires applicants who are aware that the perpetrator may be unable to read or understand information given to them all requests made to take reasonable steps to ensure and the ability to respond. It will be necessary to set out what has been done in this respect and demonstrate that it was reasonable. Most public bodies already ensure that they have recorded this information.

28. Additionally, the respondent is under 18, the Protocol reiterates that consultation should take place with the Youth Offending Team "at the earliest possible stage" but goes on to say "and in any event must take place before the application is made".

29. This appears to impose a strict obligation than is contained in the Act, which expressly excludes the need to consult when making a without-notice application. There will be few instances in which an applicant has not had time or felt it appropriate to consult the YOT, so the situation will rarely arise where a decision has to be made whether to follow the wording of the Act or the Protocol. This must be a matter of judgment for the individual officer, who will be able to justify it in their witness statement.

30. The Protocol also provides for claims against care leavers aged 18–25. Applicants will need to check whether there is a personal adviser[10] and consult, or tell the respondent of their entitlement to get one.

31. Finally if the applicant knows that the respondent is *potentially* vulnerable, and/or has mental health or capacity issues, they need to consider whether:

- the defendant has capacity to defend a claim and, if not, after consulting with the appropriate bodies, how to appoint a litigation friend;
- to direct the respondent to the NHS Liaison and Diversion Service or for other health professional;
- there are Equality Act 2010 issues;
- there is a need for a community care assessment;[11]
- steps can be taken to provide details of resources over advice and assistance to allow the respondent to participate in the proceedings fully and to give "their best evidence" if they want to do so.

32. Although such considerations were mostly included in in the Statutory Guidance, there will be more emphasis on the steps taken once the PAP comes into force. For an example of what happens when disability is not addressed properly, see Rosebery Housing Association Ltd v Williams & Anor.[12]

---

10 appointed under section 3 in skeleton arguments of the Children & Social Work Act 2017

11 Under the Care Act 2014

12 (2021) EW Misc 22 (CC), a decision of HHJ Luba, KC

33. in that case HHJ Jan Luba KC refused to make an ASBI against a disabled tenant, particularly because she had made serious allegations of her own. She suffered from OCD and had several rituals and repetitive behaviours, one of which was a compulsion to film her surroundings almost constantly. Her landlord collated over 100 allegations spanning a period of over two years. Only six sample allegations were tried, and the defendant made a counterclaim.

34. A single allegation was found proved and the landlord was not allowed to rely on the remainder of which there was evidence in the bundle, saying that a sensible approach would have been to pick six which "*would have each been the subject of clear, direct, corroborated evidence*" cross-referenced to a contemporaneous note of the victim's complaint.

35. As that did not happen, the main issue in the trial became the counterclaim for disability discrimination and the judge found that the behaviour complained of (mostly filming) was caused by her disability and the landlord "*failed to come anywhere near*" establishing that an injunction was proportionate. It had failed to follow its own ASB policy in particular by neglecting to put the 123 allegations against her at the time they were made, instead of waiting several years before deluging her. As they failed to provide information, support and encouragement of neighbour tolerance and restraint, he found they had not discharged their PSED.

36. The landlord's staff was not familiar with OCD and should have sought specialist advice on it, as a cursory risk assessment was not nearly sufficient. Other "*obvious*" lesser measures were not considered, including (somewhat surprisingly) allowing the defendant to buy the remaining interest in her home and relocate. The suggestion is that social landlords with disabled tenants should be educating themselves about mental disability and its effect on tenant interactions before seeking ASBIs. They also need to familiarise themselves with the disability legislation, particularly section 149 of the Equality Act 2010.

37. The judge saw the defendant as the victim rather than the perpetrator and awarded her £27,400 in damages (applying the *Vento* bands[13]). There would obviously have been substantial costs on top of that, so this is a lesson for all.

Pre-action steps-Part 2 of the Protocol

38. Before a decision is made to bring a claim, and applicant needs to consider whether an early intervention or alternative approach should be taken and pursue it. Evidently this cannot happen if there is an urgent need to protect a victim. If early intervention or the Statutory Guidance and Local Plan are not followed it will be necessary to explain the reasons in a witness statement (see Chapter 5).

39. Specific examples are given in paragraph 2.3, which provides a non-exhaustive list of possible reasons for failing to comply with the Protocol. Such reasons will be familiar to applicants-the need to take urgent action, to protect anyone, or where the applicant has been asked not to contact the respondent, or there has been compliance with the pre-claim conduct in relation to previous complaints.

40. Except in cases of violence or harm, potential applicants will need to contact the perpetrator and provide "full details of the allegations" so as to enable them to respond and tell them how to get legal representation or other advice.

41. This is best done by visiting the respondent or interviewing them in an office, and noting their explanations/admission/denials, then writing to them to confirm the outcome of the meeting, in compliance with paragraph 2.7 of the Protocol (see below). This process can be very useful because early admissions and explanations will help both parties, both within the injunction application and with controlling the ASB.

---

13 *Vento v Chief Constable of West Yorkshire Police* [2002] EWCA Civ 1871

42. The parties should "discuss and try to agree the steps that can be taken to address any underlying causes of anti-social behaviour." This requires the respondent to be asked whether they have any support/treatment needs and to provide written consent for the applicant to contact relevant agencies to obtain information about needs and treatment, and to provide details of solicitors who can help.

43. Paragraph 2.7 requires an applicant to write or otherwise communicate with the respondent so they will understand what steps have been agreed, timescales, the circumstances in which legal action will otherwise be taken or, if no agreement was reached, why this was so and what action will be taken.

44. All applicants will need to take reasonable steps to "establish effective ongoing liaison with appropriate support services" and, if they have consent, make contact with appropriate services before taking any decision as to enforcement.

45. The Protocol also requires applicants to consider whether the order should include any positive requirements with the aim of preventing the respondent from engaging in ASB. If so they should be identified and the supervisors selected. This information must be included in the applicant's witness statement.

Applicant's Failure to Comply with the PAP

46. The wider responsibilities mentioned in paragraph 1.4 of the PAP (para 24 above) are difficult to reconcile with. Additionally this recognition might be difficult to reconcile with paragraphs 1.6 and 3.2 of the PAP. They provide respectively that (1) the court should take into account compliance with the PAP when considering whether to make an order and, if so, its terms and (2) if the applicant *unreasonably* fails to comply with the PAP the court might impose sanctions including an order for costs or adjournment, strike out or dismissal of the claim.

47. In other words, it is only in cases where an applicant has acted unreasonably that there should be any sanction in costs.

48. However, when the court is considering marking its disapproval of a failure to comply with the PAP by, e.g., a refusal to make an order, or make one in the terms sought, the court will be careful to balance the interests of the defendant against those of the innocent victims of the ASB so as to ensure that they are protected from the defendant's conduct despite any shortcomings in following the PAP, which is unlikely to be through any fault on the part of the victims.

Respondent's unreasonable failure to comply with the protocol

49. The final paragraph of the Protocol says that the court can take into account any failure on the part of the respondent to comply with the terms of the protocol, but only in considering whether or not to grant an injunction and, if so, on what terms. For some reason there is no provision to take that failure into account in respect of costs.

Interaction between Protocol and Statutory Guidance

50. The new Statutory Guidance, revised in June 2022, contains a useful reminder that applicants should be "putting victims first", and it remains to be seen whether the Protocol is used as a foil or a spoiler in cases where there has been some failure to comply with part of it.

51. Given the obligation on public authorities to protect victims of ASB, it is to be hoped that the courts will bear in mind the purpose of the Act before imposing any sanction which interferes with the rights of victims, or imposing further burdens on public bodies which might deter them in future from taking action to reduce ASB.

CHAPTER TWO
SATISFYING THE THRESHOLD TESTS

KEY POINTS

1. Distinction between housing and non-housing related conduct
2. 'Non-housing related' conduct
3. 'Housing related' conduct
4. Location is immaterial
5. What amounts to nuisance or annoyance?
6. Nuisance or annoyance through noise
7. Non-housing related conduct
8. "Harassment, alarm or distress"
9. Gas safety injunctions and injunctions against landlords
10. The burden and standard of proof

Distinction between housing and non-housing related conduct

1. This important difference between ASB in housing related situations and in other public places was created in the final version of the 2014 Act. The House of Lords objected strongly

to the widening of the availability of the existing type of injunction to include all housing.

2. The list of bodies which have the power to apply for injunctions is wider than under the previous legislation.[14] Bodies which are faced with the need to control the behaviour of the general public are entitled to apply to the Secretary of State to be added to the list.

Non-housing related conduct

3. If the behaviour is not 'housing-related', then there is an important restriction on the circumstances in which an injunction can be obtained. It is only "*conduct that has caused, or is likely to cause, harassment, alarm or distress to any person*" (section 2 (1) (a)) that will pass the threshold:

- This is intended to make it more difficult to get an injunction for non-residential situations.
- The applicant needs either to produce a victim or prove that it is *likely* people will suffer such harm;
- After extensive consultation, the government settled on a list of potential applicants, listed in section 5 of the 2014

[14] It currently comprises local authorities, housing providers, the Police, the British Transport Police Force, Transport for London and for Greater Manchester, the West Midlands Combined Authority, the Environment Agency, the Natural Resources Body for Wales, the Secretary of State exercising security management functions, the NHS Counter Fraud Authority, the Welsh Ministers exercising security management functions, and a person or body exercising security management functions on the direction of the Welsh Ministers or under arrangements made between the Welsh Ministers and that person or body.

Act, which can be extended by order of the Secretary of State.

4. It has now been re-established by the Court of Appeal that the court can grant an injunction against Persons unknown: *London Borough of Barking and Dagenham and Others v Persons Unknown and Others.*[15]

'Housing related' conduct

5. Only local authorities and social landlords can apply for injunctions to control "housing related" ASB. The police can also use an injunction to control ASB causing a nuisance or annoyance to people's occupation of residential premises anywhere. Such applications can now be made to enforce gas (and related) safety inspection access obligations.

6. If the conduct housing related, the threshold is whether the conduct *is capable* of causing a *nuisance or annoyance in relation to a person's occupation of 'residential premises'* or (for local authorities and social landlords) in relation to the exercise of housing management functions:

    - This means that it is not necessary to produce a victim who has been caused a nuisance or annoyance.

    - Only social landlords, local authorities and the police can apply for an injunction on this basis, but it can be used against private homeowners and to protect those in privately owned accommodation.

    - Social landlords can also apply for orders when the conduct either directly or even only indirectly relates to their housing management functions, so they can protect

[15] [2022] EWCA Civ 13

employees, contractors and the like and they can apply when the conduct happens somewhere there is no social housing at all, e.g. at their offices or in shopping centres, parks etc.[16]

7. "Housing related" conduct "*can clearly be engaged in by someone who is not a tenant or an occupier of property owned by the relevant landlord; equally, it can be engaged in by someone who neither resides nor works within the area in which the conduct occurs*".[17]

8. In fact the ASB does not have to be directly related to their housing management functions-it can indirectly affect the applicant's 'administration' of their housing-a very wide phrase.

9. Housing providers apply for more injunctions than any other body. This is because the 2014 Act can address a much wider range of behaviours and the conduct does not have to be in any particular location.

Location is immaterial

10. Once that threshold is passed and the conduct can be described as "housing related", it does not matter where the conduct is happening-the perpetrator can be in social housing, private rented housing, an owner occupier, or homeless/of no fixed abode and they may be causing a nuisance or annoyance anywhere in England/Wales.

---

[16] The phrase "is a loose and broad link, emphasised by the words "directly or indirectly" and "relates to or affects" and by the merely inclusive definition of housing management functions": Rix LJ in a decision under the 1996 Act at para [38] in *Swindon BC v Redpath [2009] EWCA Civ 943, September 11, 2009; [2010] 1 All E.R. 1003*

[17] Ibid, Neuberger LJ, at [64]

What amounts to nuisance or annoyance?

11. The phrase "nuisance or annoyance" is so wide as to apply to almost any conduct, provided it fulfils that common law test. The "Statutory Guidance For Frontline Professionals" (updated December 2017) gives a few examples of what might be included: "*vandalism, public drunkenness, aggressive begging, irresponsible dog ownership, noisy or abusive behaviour towards neighbours, or bullying.*"

12. The Guidance isn't so helpful on when an order would not be appropriate, as it says they: "*should not be used to stop reasonable, trivial or benign behaviour that has not caused, or is not likely to cause, anti-social behaviour to victims or communities.*"

13. Although it should be a matter of common sense to select which incidents should be included in an application, it is often difficult to decide whether more minor incidents of ASB should be included.

14. The sensible course of action might be to make it plain that the less serious incidents are included as contextual material and to show that there has been a course of conduct. It should be stressed that they would not on their own give rise to the need for an injunction.

15. Each incident need not necessarily be so serious on its own as to be actionable in some way, as Holroyde J said in *Birmingham City Council v Pardoe* [2016] EWHC 3119: "*Anti-social behaviour will by its very nature generally involve a course of conduct. It is often the cumulative effect of anti-social behaviour over a period of time, rather than the individual acts, which causes serious harm*".

16. However, you should read the cautionary tale of *Rosebery Housing Association Ltd v Williams & Anor,*[18] in which a seemingly clear claim for an injunction was dismissed by HHJ Luba, K.C., with serious consequences for the landlord. It is a painful reminder that an applicant should never be trapped into relying on only a few of multiple allegations, although there were many other problems for the landlord.

"Nuisance and annoyance"

17. The two words really should be considered separately, because they are an alternative requirement.

Nuisance

18. The legal definition of nuisance has long been argued over in court and it includes making excessive noise by shouting, swearing or playing loud music, allowing cannabis smoke to escape from the house so as to upset neighbours, doing DIY so as to cause the walls of a neighbouring property to vibrate etc. In a housing context the phrase does not just have a technical legal meaning.[19]

Annoyance:

19. This has a wider meaning than "nuisance". The Court of Appeal defined the word "annoyance" in a case[20] about restrictive covenants in housing as whether *"reasonable people, having regard to the ordinary use of a house for pleasurable enjoyment, would be*

---

18 (2021) EW Misc 22 (CC), summarised in Nearly Legal on 16.1.22

19 *Harlow DC v Sewell* [2000] E.H.L.R. 122, where the tenant was evicted for keeping 40 cats in her house which fouled neighbouring gardens

20 *Davies v Dennis and others* [2009] EWCA Civ 1081

annoyed or aggrieved". It does not have to be a legal nuisance as defined by the common law[21].

20. The test is objective and the conduct has to be capable of being annoying to the reasonable man.[22] In *Tod-Heatley* the Court of Appeal said that "*the meaning is that which annoys, that which raises an objection in the minds of reasonable men may be an annoyance within the meaning of the covenant.*"

21. Another judge in the same case said: "*Annoyance" is a wider term than nuisance, and if you find a thing which reasonably troubles the mind and pleasure, not of a fanciful person or of a skilled person who knows the truth, but of the ordinary sensible English inhabitant of a house – if you find there is anything which disturbs his reasonable peace of mind, that seems to me to be an annoyance, although it may not appear to amount to physical detriment to comfort.*"

Nuisance or annoyance through noise

22. Noise nuisance, whether by people shouting and/or swearing within a dwelling or directed at neighbours, or the playing of music or making unreasonably loud domestic noise forms the basis of many complaints.

23. There is a difference between unreasonably expecting total silence from a neighbour and being sensitised to the activities which can be heard, so being annoyed more frequently by a neighbour who is misbehaving. A defendant may claim that the test isn't satisfied because everyday living noises can be overheard along with the nuisance.

---

[21] see the case of *Curo Places Ltd v Natalie Walker* [2018] EWHC 2462 (QB) for an example of a defendant succeeding in showing that most of the allegations were just noises of everyday living.

[22] *Tod-Heatley v Benham* (1888) 40 Ch.D 80

24. In the context of statutory nuisance under the Environmental Protection Act 1990, the High Court (Mr Justice Turner) observed in *Jones & Ors v Chapel-en-le-Frith Parish Council*[23] that *"there is no legal basis for drawing a distinction per se between noise emitted as a result of anti-social behaviour and "intended use" noise"* (i.e., noise that arises within the use of premises for a purpose permitted under planning law).

25. Equally when a complainant has been found to have become hypersensitive due to antisocial behaviour, it does not provide a defendant with a defence to say that they are suffering when others might not have done (ibid).

Contextual acts amounting to ASB

26. Further, some behaviour might only be a nuisance or annoyance when viewed in the context of other acts or omissions. This is particularly true where there is harassment (see below). It is sometimes only the cumulative effect of individual acts which causes a nuisance or annoyance, or amounts to harassment.

27. When preparing the Scott Schedule, care should be taken to separate behaviour which will fall within the definition from that which the court may find to be ordinary noises of everyday life. Often the question to ask will be whether the previous tenant made similar noise, or whether other residents in similar housing experience this type of noise.

28. The applicant has to decide what behaviour falls within the definition, what is useful background material to 'paint a picture' of what has been happening in the area in the longer term, and what facts should be included to prevent the court thinking that it hasn't been provided with a full picture.

23 [2022] EWHC 1909 (QB)

Evidence in applications without notice, powers of arrest and exclusion orders

29. The question of what evidence should be included is even more important when it comes to asking for ex-parte orders, powers of arrest and exclusion orders.

30. On a without notice application, it is essential to avoid any suggestion of a failure to make full disclosure. If there are acts which do not individually amount to ASB but do so cumulatively, this needs to be made clear, so there is no suggestion subsequently that the individual acts did not satisfy the test.

31. When asking for a power of arrest and/or an exclusion order, evidence satisfying the necessary additional tests must be included and highlighted (see Chapter Five).

Non-housing related conduct-harassment alarm or distress

32. The threshold is higher for injunctions which do not involve housing or affect housing management functions, for instance those concerning hospitals, train stations, shopping centres, public spaces, business premises and suchlike.

33. First, the behaviour must either *have already caused* harassment, alarm or distress, or it must be *likely to do so*. The possibility of such detriment is not enough, unlike the test in housing related nuisance, where the applicant only has to prove that it is *capable* of causing the detriment.

34. In practice this means that it is necessary to adduce evidence from victims themselves preferably, who can say that they have been harmed in one of the three ways. That evidence may be first-hand or hearsay, but it must be there, or alternatively there must be good evidence from a professional witness who can describe the reaction of members of the public and show that one or more of

the three requirements is satisfied, or is more likely than not to have been satisfied.

Definition of "Harassment, alarm or distress"

35. The term is the same as that used in the Public Order Act 1986 to define an offence under section 5 of that Act of using threatening, abusive or insulting words or behaviour, or disorderly behaviour and thereby causing someone else harassment, alarm or distress.

"Harassment"

36. Harassment has a statutory definition in the Protection from Harassment Act 1997 ("the 1997 Act"). The definition is wide, but the behaviour has to be more than "unattractive or regrettable", or "unreasonable and disproportionate" and has to be seen in context.[24]

37. The conduct has to be enough to satisfy the criminal test in section 2 of the 1997 Act: "*... irritations, annoyances, even a measure of upset, arise at times in everybody's day-to-day dealings with other people. Courts are well able to recognise the boundary between conduct which is unattractive, even unreasonable, and conduct which is oppressive and unacceptable. To cross the boundary from the regrettable to the unacceptable the gravity of the misconduct must be of an order which would sustain criminal liability under section 2*".[25]

38. Baroness Hale put it like this:[26]"... *the definition of harassment was left deliberately wide and open-ended. It does require a course of*

---

24 Gage LJ in *Sunderland City Council v Conn* [2007] EWCA Civ 1492, [2008] IRLR 324 at [12]

25 Lord Nicholls at [30] in *Majrowski v Guy's and Thomas's NHS Trust* [2006] UKHL 34,

26 Lady Hale in *Majrowski* at [66], cited in *Worthington and Parkin v*

conduct, but this can be shown by conduct on at least two occasions (or since 2005 by conduct on one occasion to each of two or more people): section 7(3). All sorts of conduct may amount to harassment. It includes alarming a person or causing her distress: section 7(2). But conduct might be harassment even if no alarm or distress were in fact caused. A great deal is left to the wisdom of the courts to draw sensible lines between the ordinary banter and badinage of life and genuinely offensive and unacceptable behaviour."

39. An intention to 'harass' the individual is not necessary. For instance, in *Worthington*, a housing association was found liable for damages for harassment for unjustly accusing tenants of ASB, even though it acted in good faith following complaints from many residents (see above).

40. In that case, the Housing Association ("MHT)" alleged that two tenants were using numerous CCTV cameras to film public spaces and threatened to evict them for doing so. Unfortunately, it did not confirm their facts and had failed properly to investigate the allegations it made and to gather sufficient evidence of what the tenants might be doing before making the threat. The residents responded by bringing a claim for damages for harassment.

41. The trial judge found that one of the defendants did not have any CCTV cameras and the other was merely using them for her own security and not to spy on the general public. On appeal MHT conceded that the statutory defence under section 1 (3) (c) could not apply if the conduct was properly found to be harassment.

42. The statutory defence in section 1 (3) (c) succeeds if a defendant can prove that: "… *in the particular circumstances the pursuit of the course of conduct was reasonable…*" As MHT was not acting maliciously and was merely responding to the apparently genuine

---

Metropolitan Housing Trust [2018] EWCA Civ 1125 at [6]

concerns of a large number of other residents, it is a little difficult to understand why that concession was made. The defence applies when conduct which might otherwise be harassment has a reasonable explanation.

43. Behaviour which qualifies as harassment will equally convince a court to find ASB in the form of nuisance or annoyance, whereas the reverse will not suffice.

"Alarm or distress"

44. Much is to be gained from looking at the context in which behaviour occurs. For instance, in public spaces there may be protesters aggrieved at some issue who voice their opinions loudly:[27] *"Protest is lawful; the use of a megaphone as an adjunct of lawful protest is itself lawful. The starting point is unfettered freedom to engage in so much amplified protest as is neither intimidating or harassing."*

45. So defendants might argue that while their conduct might be a nuisance or annoying to people, it doesn't intimidate or harass them. Arguably it is easier to satisfy the threshold of "distressing" somebody, although that distress must be objectively capable of being experienced. The behaviour must be likely to distress someone (which could be evidenced by a professional), or to have actually caused distress (which requires evidence from a victim).

46. The question was also considered in the context of protests in the case of *Birmingham CC v Afsar (No 3)*,[28] in which Mr Justice Warby found that the freedom of expression is not absolute and should be balanced against the rights of others. He said (at

---

27 Mr Justice Holland at paragraph 28 of his judgement *in Huntingdon Life Sciences Group Plc and Another v Stop Huntingdon Animal Cruelty* [2007] EWHC 522 (QB),

28 [2019] EWHC 3217 (QB)

paragraph 32): "*there is no reason to doubt that in passing this legislation Parliament intended to confer power to seek and to grant injunctions to prohibit anti-social utterances and assemblies of all kinds, in any case where it is shown that this is necessary and proportionate in pursuit of one of the legitimate aims identified in Articles 10(2) and 11(2). The safeguards for the human rights of protestors lie in the Court's statutory duty under s 6 of the HRA, and in the procedures of the Court.*"

47. The Bill was amended to protect behaviour which might annoy some people but was thought not to be worthy of condemnation through the legal process, such as carol singing and trick or treating. The difference is easy to see in this context-if some children turn up at a door dressed in Halloween costumes they may well irritate some people. It would be a different matter if adults dressed as characters from a horror movie and acting accordingly were to start visiting people-this could easily tip the balance and be seen as causing "alarm or distress".

Gas safety and other access injunctions

48. In an appeal by Swindon Borough Council in August 2021 His Honour Judge Michael Berkley held in a detailed judgment that the 2014 Act can be used to enforce a tenant's obligation to allow access. The judgment is likely to prove very useful to landlords attempting to obtain access to properties to inspect for gas and other safety issues.

49. In that case, Swindon Borough Council had been refused such an injunction at first instance by a Deputy District Judge. The Council appealed. The judge allowed the appeal and confirmed that the 2014 Act can be used in place of a Part 8 claim for breach of tenancy to obtain an injunction. This obviously significantly cuts costs and preparation time for a social landlord.

50. That injunction can (1) prohibit the tenant from refusing access for any inspection pursuant to the tenancy which otherwise

satisfies the threshold test for the grant of an order and (2) if necessary, require the tenant to do certain things, such as permit access in a particular way. A power of arrest can be attached if necessary.

51. The judge found that "housing related functions" as referred to in the 1996 Act had, in *Swindon BC v Redpath*[29], been interpreted widely by the Court of Appeal (and referred to with approval in *Birmingham City Council v Sharif*[30]) and their "housing management functions easily embrace its sense of responsibility to its continuing tenants".

52. He also found that the defendant's behaviour did fall within section 2 of the Act, because if neighbours found out that Mr Wood had refused to allow a gas safety inspection it was likely to cause them either (1) harassment, alarm or distress or (2) nuisance or annoyance. Such conduct was either "likely to" or "capable of" causing those defects with no need for evidence of it having taken place in fact.

53. The council had also adduced in evidence in a statement from a senior officer that it could face regulatory action and a potential fine for, and the impact of publicity over the fine would cause it nuisance and annoyance. The continued refusal to permit access, requiring the sending of multiple letters in carrying out numerous visits had involved unnecessary expenditure and use of officer time, also likely to have caused nuisance, and to have interfered with the housing related functions.

54. Equally, officers who had attended but had been refused entry were likely to have been caused a nuisance. Finally, he found that living near a property which had a potentially unsafe and untested

---

29 [2010] EWCA Civ 943

30 [2019] EWHC 1268

gas supply was likely to cause distress or nuisance, particularly given recent events. Such events speak for themselves, he said.

55. The judgment has not been well-publicised and it will no doubt take time for this confirmation of the ability to use the Act to permeate through to landlords and to judges.

Injunctions against landlords

56. Camden Council and the Metropolitan police have secured what is probably the first injunction against a landlord[31], and the various cases involving the individual deserve a look. He has been the subject of a multitude of claims, both made by and against him involving harassment of tenants, and he has made a number of claims for unlawful eviction in respect of properties at which he has never lived[32].

57. This further extension of their ambit of injunctions is likely to prove useful to social landlords attempting to address the significant rise in instances of unlawful evictions by private landlords.

The burden and standard of proof

58. The burden is on the applicant to prove the constituent requirements. While the 1996 Act only imposed the civil standard of proof, applications for the grant of an ASBO faced the tougher standard of proof "beyond reasonable doubt", the same as in the criminal courts.[33]

---

31 *Camden Council v Mohammed Ali Abbas Rasool,* (23.6.21) at the RC J

32 E.g. Rasool v Paddington Company One Ltd (2021) EWHC 3633 (QB), in which he was caught out and the judge referred to various other applications, all discussed by Giles Peaker in Nearly Legal on 13.2.22

33 *Clingham v Royal Borough of Kensington and Chelsea, R v McCann* [2002]

59. Defendants made capital of the higher standard of proof and there was inevitably a fight to prove the threshold for the imposition of an order, particularly because they were dealt with mostly in the Magistrates' Courts. Applications for gang related injunctions under the Policing and Crime Act 2009 and under the 2014 Act do not require proof to the criminal standard.[34]

UKHL 39

34 *Jones v Birmingham City Council* [2018] EWCA Civ 1189

CHAPTER THREE
IS IT 'JUST AND CONVENIENT'?

KEY POINTS

1. The basis of the test
2. Relevance to applications without notice
3. Applying the test at the on-notice hearing
4. Preparing a Scott Schedule as a checklist
5. Postscript: Mistakes can have consequences in costs

1. Once the applicant is satisfied that there has been behaviour which qualifies as anti-social within the meaning of section 1 of the 2014 Act, it is important to move on and consider whether it is "just and convenient" to make an injunction.

Basis of the test

2. This phrase has intentional echoes of the case law which governs the grant of injunctive relief in the Superior Courts Act 1981 and the common law. It is an issue which needs to be addressed separately in the application, with good evidence.

3. The question is, "*whatever technical merits there may be, is it right, is it just, is it fair to grant the injunction sought?*".[35] It is a question which has to be specifically considered by the applicant in the context of the timing and nature of any application and a policy may well explicitly require its consideration.

Relevance to applications without notice

4. It is all the more important when making an application without notice, where the court is likely to look carefully at the question in the context of the restrictions imposed on such applications by case law.

5. In those circumstances, a clear objective assessment needs to be made as to whether to apply without informing the defendant and, if so, what sort of injunction should be requested. It can be difficult to do this at the time the application is contemplated and prepared, particularly at first hearing.

6. That decision must be taken not on the basis of the evidence available, but on that which *might* be available by the return date or at the final hearing. At an interim without notice hearing, the court will nearly always be pushed for time. In any event, with only one party present, it is sometimes easy to overlook issues relevant to this question.

7. Failure to address this question can have negative consequences for an applicant. There is a 'duty of full disclosure' when making an interim application without notice. This is discussed in Chapter Seven.

---

[35] *Jbarco Investments Ltd v Omar* [2014] EWHC 4682 (QB)

Applying the test at the on-notice hearing

8. On the return hearing and on any on notice application, the court should look at this limb carefully with the benefit of a longer period of time in which to consider it. Often there is much more factual background available and the defendants' point of view will be voiced by them.

9. It is sensible to ask whether it is "just and convenient" first to apply for the order at all, then whether to apply with or without notice and finally whether to apply for any particular terms, both at the first hearing and subsequently.

10. In a 2016 decision Mr Justice Holroyd[36] gave some guidance on consideration of the phrase at paragraph 38:

> *"Turning to the second stage of the court's consideration, it would again be very surprising if the court in considering whether it was just and convenient to grant an injunction were required to ignore evidence which was logically highly relevant to that decision. As the judge rightly pointed out, evidence of conduct prior to 23rd September 2014 might militate either in favour of or against the granting of an injunction. If there was evidence to prove that a respondent had repeatedly behaved in an anti-social manner over a long period of time, and had done so despite warnings from police officers and local authority officials, that might be a strong reason for the court to grant an injunction. If on the other hand the evidence showed that the recent anti-social behaviour had occurred at a time when the respondent was subject to specific stresses in his personal life, and stood in marked contrast to a long history of being an exemplary neighbour, that might be a strong reason for the court to conclude that it would not be just or convenient to make him subject to an injunction. In short, it would be*

[36] *Birmingham City Council v Glenn Pardoe* [2016] EWHC 3119 (QB)

surprising if Parliament had intended the court to decide what was just and convenient without taking into account conduct which, although occurring some time ago, was relevant to that evaluative judgment."

11. Examples of when the court might make an anxious enquiry into the justification for any injunction at all might include:

- the ASB comprised only one (albeit perhaps serious) incident and there is no chance of repetition or more incidents have occurred but the behaviour has stopped
- there are limited allegations and they are not sufficiently serious to justify part or all of the order
- the allegations concern only the everyday noises of domestic life and the victim is unduly sensitive
- the defendant can show a change of behaviour so that an order is unnecessary
- the applicant has not followed its own procedures and has failed to consider alternatives to an injunction
- the applicant has behaved in a manner which causes the court to find that an order should not be made
- there is 'bad blood' between the witnesses and defendant or the applicant has otherwise behaved badly or there is good evidence that they have lied
- the victim has moved away
- there has been substantial delay since the last problem and there is reason to believe that a further recurrence is unlikely

12. Some of these situations deserve individual examination.

The behaviour was an isolated incident or has stopped

13. If there was only one incident and there is unlikely realistically to be a repeat, it is unlikely that an injunction will be necessary and no application is likely to be made.

14. However if the behaviour has stopped (and provably so) before an injunction is applied for, it may still be just and convenient to grant the injunction and an explanation needs to be provided in the evidence. In this context, there is no historical time limit for allegations-the court can be asked to look at ASB over the course of many years in appropriate circumstances (see the next Chapter).

15. A defendant is unlikely to be able to argue that a final injunction should not be made if the behaviour stops after the grant of an interim injunction. When a defendant applicant for housing had sent a string of offensive emails to local authority employees, the authority had applied for an injunction against him.[37] The court made an interim order and the emails stopped. The court found that despite the lack of any continuing problem, a final injunction was still appropriate. The judge said that "*the probability and indeed overwhelming likelihood is that the behaviour has only ceased because of the injunction, and the sanctions that flow from the breach of an injunction.*"

16. There are likely to be circumstances where defendants will argue that the behaviour has ceased for other reasons. If there is any suggestion of this, it needs to be addressed in evidence.

17. Even if a final injunction is not appropriate and, for instance, no order is made for an undertaking is accepted, the initial

[37] *Reigate and Banstead BC v Walsh* [2017] EWHC 2221 (QB)

application might well have been justified and the defendant may still be liable in costs to the applicant.

18. It is not enough for a defendant to say that other means could have been used to address the behaviour, provided the applicant has made a reasoned decision as to why an injunction is appropriate and that reasoning is capable of being sustained.

There are limited allegations and they are not sufficiently serious to justify part or all of the order

19. Perhaps the best way of considering this is to look at a past case[38] in which the most extreme form of order available was sought against two families, on without notice hearing. The court granted both an injunction and an exclusion order at 12:30 PM on a Friday, and then the order was only served at 9 PM.[39] In fact, the defendants did not obey the exclusion order that night and remained in their homes.

20. Over a decade later, this case is still being cited by defendants in many injunction applications. While the court has to consider fairness of the grant of an order separately from the nature of the terms, the question for the court is often not whether an order should be made at all, but what the terms of that order should be.

21. Looking at the decision in the cold light of day and with the benefit of hindsight, it is easy to identify the genesis of the challenges that were subsequently made to the grant of the order. They form a useful checklist on whether it might be "just and

---

38 *Moat Housing Limited v Harris & Hartless* [2005] EWCA Civ 287

39 This in itself is worthy of comment. If the landlord had been able to produce drafts and amend and print them at court, the orders could have been ready for signing and stamping almost immediately and could at least have been served in the afternoon when solicitors were still open. Instead the court only released the orders over three hours after the hearing, around 3 PM and it then took over three hours to serve them.

convenient" to ask for an order. What appears below might form the starting point for possible issues relating to the 'just and convenient' question.

22. The injunction application was made against two families, Mr Harris and Ms Hartless (who had four children) and "the D family", (who had six children). The Court of Appeal intimated at the start of the judgement that most of the complaints related to the D family, who formed no part of the appeal.

23. The appeal was advanced on the basis that the appellants were to an extent innocent victims of the legal process. The Court of Appeal seems to have accepted that premise and framed their judgement accordingly, despite upholding parts of the injunction. Brooke LJ said that it was apparently clear to a solicitor instructed by Ms Hartless on the night the order was made that "*the vast majority of the evidence related to a quite different family*".

24. A careful examination of the facts shows that this may have been factually accurate, but that there was still a significant amount of evidence against the appellants. If they had been the only defendants, an injunction could still have been made on that evidence. The evidence against them and/or their children of serious ASB appears to have been plentiful (see paragraphs 26-56 of the judgement). There was even an unpleasant incident involving Mr Harris and Ms Hartless during the week before the injunction application.

25. It appears that the other "D" family (who did not appeal) felt they had been quite rightly targeted for legal action. A week after the injunction was served, they left the area, never to return. They surrendered their tenancy before the trial of the possession proceedings a month later and provided undertakings as to their behaviour.

26. This might suggest that it could have been 'just and convenient' to grant the highly intrusive exclusion order against the D family, although not perhaps without notice. However, particularly where families are involved, it is rarely likely to be appropriate to ask for an exclusion order without notice. These days such an injunction is highly unlikely to be made.

27. Careful consideration needs therefore to be given to exactly what each defendant is alleged to have done, or how they are said to have encouraged or permitted which particular conduct by others. Often it will not be a case of whether it is just and convenient to make an application for an injunction at all, but whether the application in respect of each defendant should be made without notice and what relief should be requested. That question needs to be considered separately for each potential defendant and care needs to be taken to distinguish draft orders appropriately between defendants.

Everyday noises of domestic life

28. Defendants will often say that the neighbour is not entitled to complain about the noises of ordinary existence. There is obviously a difference between such noises and unreasonable behaviour constituting a nuisance and annoyance. It is important to distinguish the two and to collect evidence to rebut this defence before it is raised.

29. Any family of parents and children will generate significantly more disturbance than a retired couple and many social landlords administer their estates by reference to age brackets in accommodation.

30. Family life begins to be a nuisance when an occasional argument becomes constant, aggressive verbal and/or physical fights. Occasionally shouting at children is different to swearing or behaving aggressively towards them. Care must be taken to address this issue, with good evidence, preferably corroborated by

more than one neighbour. Alternatively one neighbour can record the sounds being generated.

A defendant can change their behaviour for the better

31. Infrequently, a defendant can show that they were going through a 'bad patch' and they have improved their behaviour of their own volition, for instance by giving up alcohol or drugs, or by going to anger management or splitting up with an aggressive partner.

ASB policies are not followed

32. It might not be just and convenient to make an injunction if a defendant has not had sufficient notice that their behaviour was being challenged. This issue is likely to take centre stage following the introduction of the Protocol, as it is part of the required pre-action conduct on the part of the applicant.

33. Before the application was issued in the *Moat Housing* case, apparently Ms Hartless had not been warned that she was in breach of tenancy, or that her children had misbehaved. This is almost unheard of and would today be in breach of most ASB policies and soon the PAP. Such a breach would need careful explanation, which might be that a serious incident has occurred and a warning is not appropriate. Even in such a case, it is necessary to show there is a likelihood of repetition of that behaviour, or of intimidation of witnesses etc.

34. Absent any such explanation, it is likely that if proceedings are brought without warning against an individual, they will defend the claim saying that it is not just and convenient to grant an injunction when other methods of control have not been attempted.

The applicant's conduct is relevant generally

35. In a case which involved a freezing order rather than ASB,[40] the High Court emphasised the importance of this second limb of the test. The judge in that case discharged the interim injunction because he did not find the first limb of the requirement satisfied. He further said that even if he had found that there was a good arguable case, he would have given "*active consideration*" to whether it was just and convenient to continue the injunctive relief, given the way the applicant had conducted itself.

36. This might be particularly so if an applicant fails to comply with the duty of full disclosure (see Chapter Five on preparation of applications). But it should be an unusual step for a judge to take where the true losers in such a situation would be the innocent victims of ASB.

Bad blood and counter-allegations

37. Most applicants are not likely to be taken in by ill-founded complaints by people with a grudge. However, it can happen that there is victimisation of an individual, which can have serious results. The reasons for any complaints, the background of complainants, their behaviour in other tenancies etc. are all relevant in assessing whether there is any danger that action is being contemplated on behalf of the wrong party.

38. Equally, the existence of counter-allegations must be drawn to the attention of the court at the first hearing. It may be appropriate to bring proceedings against both families, with evidence from others not involved.

39. If a decision is made to proceed against one family only, an explanation should be provided of why the applicant has sided

---

40 *Jbarco Investments Ltd v Omar* [2014] EWHC 4682 (QB)

with those individuals. It is necessary to assess the strength of evidence in respect of all the allegations, and to search for corroboration either way.

Victim has moved away

40. If it was a squabble between two otherwise reasonable people, this might be a reason to refuse relief. In reality this is rarely the case and victims often move away rather than trying to defeat the perpetrator. Sometimes it may be appropriate to pursue an injunction for the protection of others, relying on the evidence of a witness who is no longer in the area.

41. In such a case, the applicant will need to ensure that there is reason that the court should conclude that the ASB is likely to continue if not controlled by an injunction.

Delay and no prospect of repetition

42. Again, few applicants will bring proceedings where there is an explicable and temporary worsening of behaviour on the part of a defendant. However, occasionally perpetrators will abstain from causing a nuisance in the run-up to a hearing. Care must be taken if they might wrongly persuade the court that they have reformed. An adjournment of the application might be a backstop if there is no alternative.

Preparing a Scott Schedule as a checklist

43. In simple cases, with only a few allegations against a single individual, a Scott Schedule may not appear to be necessary. However, even the clearest cases may only appear simple to the person who is preparing them.

44. The first judge who looks at the application will no doubt have limited time. The papers may not be exactly in order. If they can look at a schedule which tells them where each allegation is

evidenced, preferably by paragraph number, they are more likely to find the relevant evidence and be inclined to agree with the applicant. Additionally, that same document can and should highlight the allegations which justify the power of arrest and exclusion order if sought.

45. Therefore, a Schedule should be drafted at the same time the application is prepared. This also means that the applicant will be alive to the nature of the allegations against each person, when they occurred, what evidence exists to prove those allegations and therefore what type of injunction should be sought. Often it also becomes clear whether there is enough evidence to apply without notice and on which terms of the injunction a power of arrest should be sought.

46. Reading the judgement in *Harris and Hartless*, it would appear that no schedule was prepared by the claimant. Given the number of allegations set out in the judgement, even if the D family had not been involved at all, it is clear that some swift action needed to be taken to address the behaviour of Harris, Hartless and their children.

47. However, a schedule might well have caused the landlord to realise that an application for an exclusion order without notice was ill-advised, or that it needed to be clear which evidence justified immediate action and what form of remedy should be sought in respect of each defendant. Perhaps the claimant or the District Judge would have seen a distinction between the D family and Harris and Hartless and only excluded one family or one of the partners. As it was, she made immediate exclusion orders against both and the result was a very expensive appeal.

48. Even if no schedule is prepared, it is a good idea to set out in a separate single page document in any event the factual justification for going without notice and for a power of arrest. This should refer specifically to facts by listing the relevant paragraph numbers of witness statements.

Postscript: Mistakes can have consequences in costs

49. The aftermath of *Moat Housing*[41] provides a salutary warning about getting things right first time. Normally a defendant in an injunction application will be unable to pay the claimant's costs. If a defendant is legally aided, even if successful the claimant cannot recover them without detailed assessment of the defendant's means. Nearly every defendant has little income and the costs are rarely paid, because claimants often balk at making an application to recover them at the rate of a few pounds a week.

50. When parties appeal to the Court of Appeal, the costs will be significant. In *Moat Housing* the costs consequences of those appeals were serious for both the MHT which had to pay the defendant appellants' costs of the appeal and the first firm of solicitors which represented the defendants, who did not get paid anything for their work.

51. The appellants had switched solicitors partway through the appeal. The second firm of solicitors sent their bill to MHT, who agreed in overall figure for the possession and injunction appeals. The MHT agreed to pay the second firm of solicitors a total of £48,175 for the appeals, which the association subsequently paid, making it a very expensive injunction.

52. Meanwhile the first firm which represented both appellants then submitted a bill to MHT of £53,127 (they were working on a conditional fee agreement). MHT objected to paying it and the court upheld their objection, meaning that the solicitors received nothing for the work they did defending the claim before the second firm took over from them.

---

41 *Harris & Anor v Moat Housing Group-South Ltd* [2007] EWHC 3092 (QB) and [2008] EWHC 90098 (Costs)

CHAPTER FOUR
GATHERING EVIDENCE

KEY POINTS

1. Introduction
2. Urgent cases: oral evidence before preparation of a witness statement
3. 'First-hand' evidence
4. Witness statements
5. Complying with the CPR
6. Contents of the statement
7. Evidence from victims
8. Evidence from the defendant
9. Scott Schedules
10. Hearsay evidence
11. Evidence as the claim develops
12. Identification evidence
13. Special measures-section 16
14. Data protection/GDPR

Introduction

1. Readers of this book may have some experience of evidence collection and know that a wide variety of different sources can be used.

2. The most obvious distinction between the types of evidence is (1) oral evidence contained in witness statements and (2) the documentary or other exhibits attached to those statements. The second distinction is between evidence provided first-hand by a witness and 'hearsay' evidence.

Urgent cases: oral evidence before preparation of a witness statement

3. In some urgent cases, an application may be made without notice because a serious incident has occurred which demands immediate action, before any paperwork can be prepared. Such applications are usually made by telephone and the court provides for them to be made out of hours if necessary.

4. On those applications the court will accept the oral evidence of witnesses, either brought to court or even on the telephone.

5. Even if you are thinking of making an application which is so urgent that you do not have time to draft any documents, there should be some corroborative documentation that you can file at court electronically, and/or bring to court to substantiate your oral evidence, e.g. police statements, photographs, CCTV etc.

6. At the ex-parte hearing, the court should order the provision of written evidence within a certain time, which is likely to be after service of the order. A note must be taken of what is said at the hearing, and particularly the evidence which the court heard. This should be provided to the defendant. Sometimes it will be appropriate to obtain and serve a transcript of the whole hearing.

'First-hand' evidence

7. For reasons which should be obvious, first-hand evidence of a victim or other witness given from the witness box is the best method of proving any factual allegations.

8. Additionally, such evidence should be supported by contemporaneous documents. Witnesses may have nuisance logs, emailed reports of each incident, or may have recorded ASB on a mobile phone or using a nuisance App. All such evidence will reduce the ability of a defendant to challenge the claim on the facts.

9. No evidence should be rejected just because it is not given first-hand. Anything that is relevant and probative can and should be used and if it's hearsay it should be included in the statement of the person best placed to give it. Generally, the louder a defendant complains about the admission of evidence, the more probative and prejudicial to their case it is likely to prove.

Witness statements

10. It is surprisingly difficult to draft witness statements which both comply with the CPR and which provide all the necessary evidence in a form which is easily understood by the court. Evidence which fails in any material respect to live up to the required standard detracts from the application.

11. While the court will not expect the maker of a witness statement to use perfectly grammatically correct English, it is easy to imagine how each mistake might add to the irritation of a busy judge who has been asked to deal with an unwelcome additional application.

12. A few simple guidelines on grammar and formatting:

    - use apostrophes properly;

- avoid unnecessary words (e.g. "on 8.9.18" not "on the 8th September 2018");

- use simple rather than pompous words (e.g. "helped" rather than "assisted", "told" rather than "advised" etc);

- get the case right (e.g.: "… the defendant contacted me…", not: "… the defendant contacted myself…");

- summarise conversations which are more fully noted in a contemporaneous record exhibited to the statement. Include only the most prejudicial and probative evidence, leaving the peripheral to the exhibit. At the same time ensure that material which is helpful to the defendant is mentioned;

- make sure the statement is 'topped and tailed' correctly- follow the exact format required by the CPR, particularly CPR 32.8 PD 32 on formatting, exhibits and statements of truth;

- use automatic paragraph numbering when drafting and ensure that it is mostly chronological, though in cases where there is a 'trigger' incident that should be dealt with first, along with the reasons for an ex-parte application;

- set out the facts relied on support of the power of arrest in respect of each clause;

- get someone else involved in the case to proof-read and suggest additions/alterations.

13. Some of these are addressed in more detail below. The combined effect of a number of otherwise minor drafting errors, omissions or mistakes gives the impression that the applicant does not know what they are doing. The court can lose confidence in the claimant and be hesitant about granting the order sought, or at least all of the relief.

14. The example witness statement in Appendix A shows one possible version of a witness statement which complies with the rules and contains the material which the District Judge will need to give them jurisdiction to grant the order.

Complying with CPR 32 and PD 32, paragraphs 17-23

Identifying the Statement

15. The standard form of witness statement specified in the rules contains sensible requirements which make it easier to identify the maker of the statement, its place in the claim, the date it was made and how many exhibits are attached. Every witness statement must contain those details in the top right-hand corner. Ensure they are changed for every statement.

Body of the Statement

16. The body of the witness statement needs to comply with other requirements which are equally helpful to the court: they concern font size, line spacing, the identification of exhibits, paragraph numbering and the like.

Statement of Truth

17. The Statement of Truth must comply with the requirements of CPR 32.8 and PD 32.20.1-3 and PD 22 and 3A. If a witness statement or an exhibit fails to comply with Part 32 or the PD, the court may refuse to admit it in evidence or to allow the costs arising from its preparation and permission will need to be sought from the judge in the court where the case is proceeding.[42]

[42] CPR PD 32.25

18. The statement is not admissible as evidence unless the Statement of Truth is signed or the court has excused signature for some reason.

Identifying Exhibits

19. Use the phrase "There is now produced and shown to me, marked "**Exhibit XY/1**" a copy of ....(whatever)". In theory the exhibit number should be marked in the margin of the witness statement, but in practice nobody ever does so and it's never picked up.

Contents of the statement

Direct, First-Hand Evidence

20. There are essential facts of which evidence needs to be given in any application, depending on the identity of the deponent. A victim will need to say how they fall within the definition of those the 2014 Act can protect.

21. There is an ideal way to frame such witness statements and a template for a witness statement is included in the Appendix.

Supporting/corroborating evidence for the basic facts

22. It is necessary to provide the best possible supporting evidence of the facts relied on and, if that is not available, explain why not and why other hearsay evidence can safely be relied upon.

23. In any application there are certain basic facts which need to be proved. For instance:

- a housing provider should ideally exhibit evidence that they have title to a property or have been appointed to manage it by the freehold owner. Ensure that the proceedings are issued in the name of the relevant social landlord or freeholder, not for instance in the name of the management company.

- The contract under which someone occupies housing needs to be exhibited, although often this can cause a witness statement to be unduly bulky. To keep the witness statement to a more manageable size, it is possible to exhibit only the pages which are relevant and to state that the remainder of the agreement will be disclosed and has in any event been provided to the defendant upon taking up the tenancy.

- Evidence of any policies or procedures which have been followed should be given and this may include exhibiting the relevant provisions.

- Evidence supporting the allegations can be exhibited to a housing provider witness statement, because there will be records of complaints made.

- Equally, once complaints have been made, evidence of what the housing provider has done in response to the complaint is and highly relevant. When the PAP comes into force, material will need to be included proving compliance with its terms. Often there is a sequence to which a landlord can point of incidents and responses, which will form the basis of compliance with the PAP. However, in serious and urgent cases there may be little or no record of past problems and therefore no alternatives to legal proceedings may have been attempted. The PAP provides for this possibility.

- Evidence of what other agencies have done or attempted to do with a defendant need to be exhibited. Social Services can sometimes provide highly relevant evidence, although they may take the view that their duty of confidentiality prevents them from disclosing certain evidence. If they do, they can be made the subject of a witness summons, dealt with elsewhere in the book.

- Particularly where the history is long and complex, it is beneficial if the lead witness goes through the chronological history of ASB, e.g. if there are multiple victims alleging different incidents. Each allegation made has to be set out clearly, not as a hearsay report, but stating what happened. The source of the allegation should be included in brackets after each incident, including any page number if referring to exhibits.

- If hearsay evidence is being used, the witness needs to go into as much detail as possible as to why that material is credible and should be given as much weight as oral evidence.

- It is necessary to be clear about the effect the ASB has had on victims. Medical evidence should be obtained if at all possible. Otherwise, if a victim has taken time off work, a letter can be obtained from the employer confirming that it was because they reported sick because of nights disturbed by ASB.

- A final paragraph needs to be included summarising why the claim is made.

- If an application for an injunction is being made ex-parte, the reason why should be explained, and if a power of arrest is sought, it will be necessary to set out the incidents relied upon in support of the application.

Evidence from victims

24. Although the 2014 Act allows an applicant to bring injunctive proceedings without evidence from any victims at all, in almost every case there is some material.

25. That can be in the form of witness statements from named individuals (with those names redacted if necessary), or statements from anonymous witnesses (which only ever contained a name such as "witness X"). Those witnesses can give evidence in court if it is possible to persuade them to do so. They can remain anonymous even though they step into the witness box through the use of witness protection measures.

26. Often, if a potential witness knows that they are alone in being asked to give evidence, they will be more reluctant. It may be possible to arrange a meeting of residents not to discuss their evidence (which would prejudice the case) but to talk about whether some or all of them will give evidence and, if not, what type of witness statements they are prepared to give.

27. First-hand evidence is given more weight by corroborative evidence, such as:

- log sheets/nuisance diaries (made while the matter was 'fresh in the mind' of the maker)
- video footage
- sound recordings
- other witnesses saying the same thing
- emails to the landlord/police/EHO etc
- emails from/to other victims
- convictions of the defendant for criminal acts
- police call logs
- MG 11 incident records

- evidence from the EHO, e.g. sound recordings taken by them

28. In most cases there is likely to be a selection of the above corroborative material.

29. The Police will nearly always have helpful and relevant evidence on their files, and obtaining this material should be a priority, as it is often frustrating and difficult to do despite the information sharing obligations on the service. The GDPR have made it even more of a challenge than it already was under the DPA.

30. In rare cases, where the allegation is one of frequent and sustained noise nuisance, e.g. by the playing of loud music or continual DIY, the EHO may have become involved. Sometimes that results in a permanent solution to the problem, particularly if sound equipment is seized and confiscated by them. If the nuisance continues and injunction proceedings are started, EHO recordings can be very helpful, although this is in practice rare.

Evidence from the defendant themselves

31. Many applicants forget or neglect to interview a potential defendant. This can be important for a number of reasons and with the coming into force of the Protocol, will be fundamental:

    - There is a duty of fairness to ask a potential defendant for their version of events and to explore whether the victims are telling the truth, to test the evidence obtained.

    - Depending on what the defendant says, there may well be reason to try to support them, e.g. because they are themselves being harassed, because they have a drug or alcohol issue which they are prepared to address, or children in their care are out of control despite their best efforts and they want help.

- A defendant may well admit conduct when it has just happened, whereas months or even years later they may have forgotten the incident, or just deny it anyway because they know that otherwise there will be negative consequences.

- An admission in interview can mean that a potential witness need not give evidence, although if there is a divergence between the two accounts it is likely to be necessary to call the victim. Witnesses should be asked to comment in a further statement if a conflict between their evidence and the defendant's version arises.

32. Additionally, the defendant may have telephoned or written to the claimant with their explanation of events, or a contemporaneous complaint. Such records are disclosable in any event, but may yield useful evidence.

Scott Schedules

33. The applicant's sources of evidence should fit together like a jigsaw. Each strand should be capable of being identified in respect of each allegation in a 'Scott Schedule', by reference to a named witness and paragraph number, or by bundle page number.

34. A defendant may allege that material has been made up, or that it is too general, factually less than 100% accurate (e.g. mistakes in colour clothes/car/make of car/identity of others with defendant). Cross-referencing can help to pick this up so reasons for apparent inconsistencies can be found. Corroboration helps a judge to be satisfied that facts are not made up or inaccurate.

35. It is always possible victims may be lying or exaggerating and investigations must always bear this in mind, even when they are advanced and action has been taken. The possibility of a 'victim'

making a pre-emptive strike by reporting to the police or a landlord their version of an incident in which they in fact were the aggressor must be considered and discounted if there is any suggestion from the putative defendant.

36. If material comes into the claimant's hands which causes it to doubt the veracity of allegations, or the credibility of the witness, it must be investigated and recorded. If relevant and possibly helpful to the defendant/prejudicial to the case, it must be disclosed.

37. The collection of evidence tends to become more difficult with increasingly unpleasant conduct. The more frightening a defendant, the less likely it is that anyone will give a first-hand, named statement describing the ASB in detail.

Hearsay evidence

38. Hearsay of any sort is admissible in all civil cases and evidence cannot be excluded just because it is not given first-hand by a witness in court. This provision is particularly important in ASB law. It is surprising that some judges are still wary of giving such evidence the weight it deserves, despite the fact that the Civil Evidence Act 1995 ("the 1995 Act") has now been in force for over 20 years.

39. It is essential to be familiar with the wording of the 1995 Act and to be able to prepare the hearsay evidence and to defend any hearsay on which the applicant is relying with reference both to the words of the statute and the resulting case law.

40. It is also worth reading the Law Commission report which recommended this Act and the sea-change in the laws of evidence which it brought about.[43]

[43] The Law Commission Publication "The Hearsay Rule in Civil

41. Hearsay evidence can either be given in the witness statements of individuals, or in statements or documents provided by individuals who are not giving evidence at all. The fundamental difference between hearsay contained in a witness statement and that which it is intended to adduce without calling any witness is the requirement of notice.

42. If a party is intending to rely on hearsay but not to call the witness who has included it in their statement, notice of that intention must be given[44] to the other side. The onus is then on the receiving party to ask about the evidence so they can respond to it.

43. If one party serves a notice, the other side may apply to call the maker of the statement to be cross-examined on its contents, provided they do so within 14 days of service of the notice of intention. Note that the applicant will not need to call the witness themselves, it is up to the respondent to make the application.

44. The 1995 Act makes provision for circumstances when it might not be reasonable or practicable to give any notice of the intention to adduce hearsay, for instance when there is an urgent hearing or when witnesses have been severely intimidated or threatened.

45. It is unnecessary to serve notice of intention to rely on hearsay in respect of evidence to be given at hearings other than trials.

46. If a party fails to give notice of intention to rely on the hearsay, the evidence is still admissible.[45] However, that failure may be taken into account by the court in considering the question of

Proceedings" 1993

[44] cf section 2 the 1995 Act and CPR 33.2 & 3

[45] cf section 2 (4)

costs and other orders and "*as a matter adversely affecting the weight to be given to the evidence in accordance with section 4*".

47. When collecting the evidence in the first place, it pays dividends to use as a checklist the factors set out in section 4 of the 1995 Act:

> *(1) In estimating the weight (if any) to be given to hearsay evidence in civil proceedings the court shall have regard to any circumstances from which any inference can reasonably be drawn as to the reliability or otherwise of the evidence.*
>
> *(2) Regard may be had, in particular, to the following—*
>
> *(a) whether it would have been reasonable and practicable for the party by whom the evidence was adduced to have produced the maker of the original statement as a witness;*
>
> *(b) whether the original statement was made contemporaneously with the occurrence or existence of the matters stated;*
>
> *(c) whether the evidence involves multiple hearsay;*
>
> *(d) whether any person involved had any motive to conceal or misrepresent matters;*
>
> *(e) whether the original statement was an edited account, or was made in collaboration with another or for a particular purpose;*
>
> *(f) whether the circumstances in which the evidence is adduced as hearsay are such as to suggest an attempt to prevent proper evaluation of its weight.*

48. In preparing for the final hearing and planning who is to attend court, the applicant needs to think about any circumstances

which the court might use to draw inferences as to the reliability or otherwise of the evidence.

49. Ideally, a claimant would simply call all the witnesses who have anything relevant and probative to say. In practice this is a totally unattainable ideal, even if when first interviewed they say they will attend court.

50. A defendant is likely to criticise hearsay if there is documentary proof or they can get an admission in cross-examination that:

- it would have been reasonable and practicable to get the witness to court;
- the original statement was not made at the time of the incident (and the longer afterwards it was made the greater the criticism can be made);
- there is multiple hearsay, in that someone told someone else, or another person created the record concerned;
- there is any evidence that a witness has been inconsistent, or that they have reason to lie or exaggerate about the defendant's conduct;
- the evidence has in some way been 'doctored' and what remains is not truly representative of the facts. Defendants can say that video footage does not include the beginning of an incident, or what subsequently happened. For instance they can tell the court that they were grossly provoked before the camera was switched on, or that when the 'victim' stopped recording an incident, they attacked the defendant;
- if witnesses are not being brought to court and the defendant establishes that they could have come, the defendant is likely to say that the claimant has failed to

bring them to prevent their evidence being tested in cross-examination.

51. The court will have regard to the guidance given in a number of leading cases[46] and to sections 1-7 of the 1995 Act and CPR 33.1–5.

52. *Solon* is still regularly being cited by both sides. In *Solon* the Housing Association had provided its evidence in the form of hearsay reports made in interviews and phone calls to the police and to employees. It called some live evidence but residents were too frightened to come to court and face the defendant.

53. Mance LJ discussed the best approach, which should be followed in all case preparation:

> "*It seems to me that the Judge therefore directed himself with some care in relation to the hearsay evidence. He says specifically that it was 'important to compare the hearsay evidence with the live evidence and to adopt a more restrictive view of the hearsay evidence <u>where it seems not to be consistent with the live evidence</u>'. He accepted the housing association's live evidence rather than the appellant's live evidence and he found the hearsay evidence entirely consistent with (his) findings of fact in the live evidence. He found that it fitted the pattern established by the live evidence.*"

54. Defendants can attack the hearsay evidence, relying on what Mance LJ said about assessment of the weight to be given to:

46 *Solon South West Housing Association Ltd v James [2004] EWCA Civ 1847; [2005] H.L.R. 24, CA* at 14-41; *Moat Housing Group v Harris [2005] EWCA Civ 287; [2006] Q.B. 606, CA*, applied in Cleary v Highbury Corner Magistrates' Court [2007] 1 W:R 1272 and *Incommunities Ltd v Boyd [2013] EWCA Civ 756, June 26, 2013, CA, unrep,. para37-51*. See also *Clingham v Kensington & Chelsea LBC* [2002] UKHL 39

"*there is certainly power under the CPR to exclude hearsay evidence.*" He did not think (para 18-19 of the judgement) that there is any significant difference between asking the court to exclude evidence and submitting that, under section 4 the 1995 Act, the evidence should be given little weight even if it is to be admitted.

55. Establishing a pattern of consistency with the limited available live evidence is therefore likely to satisfy the court that the evidence is credible and should be given substantial weight, even though the witnesses have not even been identified.

56. If the police officers or claimant employees happen to witness ASB of the type complained of by anonymous witnesses, it adds substantial weight to the claim. In some cases, it may be worth paying private detectives to carry out observations. This is particularly easy if there is a pattern of consistent and frequent dealing from a property. Alternatively, CCTV can be installed, or witnesses can be asked to record incidents of ASB using mobile phones or video cameras.

Impeaching credibility

57. A party can adduce evidence[47] which would be admissible for the purposes of attacking or supporting the credibility of the witness who is not being called, and evidence of inconsistent statements is also allowed. This is particularly pertinent if a witness has previous convictions or can be shown to be biased.

Anonymous hearsay evidence

58. Usually the maker of the statement should be identified and section 3 of the 1995 Act presupposes that this will be the case. However, there is nothing to stop a party from adducing evidence

[47] Section 5(2) of the 1995 Act

given by someone who is not willing to be, or cannot be identified.

59. Reluctance may arise out of fear or for some other reason and in ASB cases courts are accustomed to dealing with such a situation. If an applicant chooses not to identify witness, CPR 33.4 does not provide the defendant with any guaranteed retort, because there is no principle which prevents the court from giving such weight as it thinks fit to hearsay evidence just because the maker is identified.

60. Defendants will make strong points that the evidence cannot be tested by cross-examination if they cannot demand the attendance at court of the witness and they do not even know their identities so they have no means at all of assessing the credibility. If a defendant does raise the inability to cross-examine, a judge will need to be reminded of the need for caution and to follow the guidance given in the relevant cases.

Collecting evidence as to the fear expressed by witnesses

61. It is necessary to set out with some care why witnesses are frightened and a general assertion will not be sufficient. If possible, the witness should be tested on their concern about intimidation or there are other reasons for not wanting to attend court. If a witness has been forced to seek medical help as a result of the fear they are experiencing, a brief letter or report should be obtained from a doctor.

62. The claimant should also check its own sources to make sure that it knows nothing detrimental about witnesses. In very serious cases, where residents are terrified (particularly frequent in cases of heroin and Crack dealing defendants/'County lines' cases), the Police may be able to help.

63. The police may confirm that anonymous witnesses are people of good character and that there is no intelligence linking them to

criminal activity of any sort. A housing provider should obviously check the tenancy records of any witness to ensure that they have not themselves been involved in ASB or dishonesty. Any material prejudicial to the credibility of a witness must be disclosed.

64. Defendants may object if the witness themselves gives their opinion of whether or not the person who has given anonymous hearsay information can be trusted. A defendant might object and say that any opinion is expert evidence and therefore subject to the restrictions of CPR 35, the veracity of a witness being a matter for the court.

65. For this reason, it is essential to ensure that the witness provides factual evidence to assist the court in determining whether the hearsay should be given any substantial weight, e.g how long they have known the individual, whether the witness has ever been accused of ASB themselves, what sort of lifestyle they lead, whether the evidence is wholly consistent with other sources.

66. Sometimes this can be difficult without giving away the identity of the person who wishes to remain anonymous. It is not ideal to have to ask the court to make a leap of faith and to get a witness to say "*I have known the individual concerned for a considerable amount of time and have taken into account … (a variety of facts which can be set out in the statement) which make me believe that they are telling the truth*". If there is no alternative, then this is better than nothing and the fallout can be dealt with in evidence.

67. Often, by the time that committal proceedings are brought, an anonymous witness will be so fed up with the defendant that they will be prepared to take the risk and be named. For this reason, even if a witness has at the outset refused to be named, the claimant should return to them during the proceedings to check that is still the case.

Evidence as the claim develops

68. It is never too late to put in additional evidence. This is particularly so in the weeks leading up to any trial and especially if something happens very shortly before, during or even after the hearing but before judgement.

69. If the date for service of witness evidence has passed, further witness statements are not admissible unless the court gives permission to file them. In practice defendants' solicitors are likely to agree that further evidence should be admitted, particularly if threatened with an application for permission to adduce such evidence.

70. If a defendant refuses to agree to updating evidence, an application should be made on the basis that further ASB has occurred and it is necessary to bring the factual material up-to-date. Particularly where there has been a period of quiet before the trial, if there is nuisance in the lead up to the trial it is very important to ensure that the evidence of continuing problems is admissible.

71. Evidence can be adduced even after the claimant has closed its case, although an application needs to be made to re-open the claim to adduce further evidence.

Identification evidence

72. Every witness needs to be clear in their evidence as to identification. See *R v Turnbull* for guidance. A defendant in a case where identification is an issue may say that the witnesses are mistaken on the identification because they were too far away, was dark, they only saw the back of the defendant, they got the clothes the wrong colour, etc.

73. In a "fleeting glimpse" situation where a witness only sees someone for a few seconds, the defendant is likely to say that

without corroboration the court cannot conclude that it was the defendant. There are obvious issues on committals in this respect, but because the burden of proof is lower in the initial application, court may feel that it can conclude that it is more likely than not it was the defendant.

Special measures-section 16

74. The 2014 Act specifically allows the court to take steps to protect witnesses, in the same way that witnesses in criminal trials can give evidence without disclosure of their identity and from behind a screen or by video.

75. These measures can also be used if the witnesses identified, but they find the presence of the defendant in court to be intimidating. A screen can simply be erected to prevent the defendant from seeing the witness. Frequently the position of that screen will mean that only the judge can see the witness and the advocate will need to deal with their evidence without being able to see them.

76. An application for special measures should be made in writing well before the hearing and just before the hearing the applicant should confirm with the court staff that they have remembered to put those measures in place.

Data protection/GDPR

77. This is a somewhat fraught subject, because although the government believes in partnership working, the measures it has enacted to protect the sharing of data substantially interfere with the process.

78. Historically, before the rise of the right to privacy following the Human Rights Act, the police would invariably provide the evidence they gathered during an investigation, which would include statements by police officers and of the witnesses, copies

of exhibits/photographs and previous criminal convictions of the defendant. They would sometimes disclose intelligence information.

79. Agencies involved in the control of antisocial behaviour are entitled to share data about subjects. However, the severe penalties imposed for breach of the GDPR have had a negative effect on the exchange of information.

80. Since the coming into force of the Data Protection Act and the subsequent GDPR, the material which the police will disclose is often limited. The reasoning upon which they refuse to provide might be weak. They invariably say that disclosure might prejudice a criminal enquiry.

81. Data holders have to designate an officer to protect the data that they control. Those individuals must justify their position and therefore apply the law meticulously and often laboriously. The result is that it can be difficult to obtain relevant and probative evidence from the police, or at least to obtain it within any reasonable timeframe.

82. Those enquiries can last for many months and sometimes years and frequently they do not result in any criminal proceedings, or the charges brought do not reflect the seriousness of the conduct. This is frequently so when a drugs raid yields material which clearly evidences possession with intent to supply, but after a long investigation a plea to simple possession is accepted. In the meantime, the evidence gathered, which is very useful in a civil context, is often (wrongly) denied to the applicant for a civil injunction.

Summary

83. In any claim there will be many sources of evidence which can be put before the court. The aim should be to provide a coherent description of the ASB, corroborated as necessary.

84. Though some evidence may not look particularly important or appear to be capable of being given any significant weight, it often assumes greater relevance as matters progress, providing context or corroboration.

CHAPTER FIVE
APPLICATIONS FOR INJUNCTIONS

KEY POINTS

1. Venue-under or over 18s, or both?
2. Applications in the youth court
3. Preparing the application
4. Duty of full and frank disclosure
5. Procedural requirements
6. The witness statement(s)
7. Deciding which incidents to include in the witness statement
8. Proving facts by inference
9. Addressing disability/capacity issues at an early stage
10. 'Tidying up' the witness statement
11. Interpretation – section 20-physical and mental injury

1. When the decision has been made that there is enough material on which to bring an application for an injunction, on the identity of the prospective defendants has been decided and evidence has been collected, the application has to be prepared for the right court in the correct form.

2. It's easy to get things mostly right, but there are a few potential trip hazards on the way.

Venue-under or over 18s, or both?

3. Perpetrators over the age of 10 but under 18 are dealt with in the Youth Court. It is possible to control the behaviour of miscreants aged under 10 by the use of injunctions obtained against their carers over the age of 18.

4. There are practical and procedural differences between proceeding in that court and in the County Court. A reasoned choice needs to be made as to where to proceed where consideration is being given to obtaining an injunction against an under 18-year-old.

5. Some initial differences to consider:

   - The Youth Offending Team and other bodies involved must be consulted except in cases of real urgency (although the draft PAP says that they should be consulted "*at the earliest possible stage and in any event … before the application is made*", allowing for no exceptions in the case of urgency [48].

   - The process is likely to be more cumbersome as this results in lay justices dealing with the application, and they may not be familiar with ASBIs.

   - It is also likely to slow because a court has to be convened specially in most circumstances.

   - It has been said that some youths used to regard an ASBO as a badge of honour. Few adults regard an injunction the same way.

[48] Section 14(1)

- The maximum period for which an injunction can be granted against an under 18-year-old is 12 months, whereas an injunction against a carer can prohibit them from failing to control children for any period specified by the court and often well in excess of the year.

- Finally, if the young person does breach the junction, the sanctions are unlikely to be put into effect by the magistrates as swiftly as the adult court will deal with the carer.

- The maximum term of detention in a young offender institution for a defendant aged between the minimum 14 and 18 is only 3 months[49], so a youth will only ever serve six weeks or less.

- Detention can only be imposed if the court is satisfied that "in view of the severity or extent of the breach, no other power available to the court is appropriate".

- Before making an application for a supervision or detention order the applicant must consult the appropriate YOT and inform any other body or individual it thinks appropriate, and consider representations received.

- The alternative remedy available is a supervision order under Part 2 of Schedule 2.

6. As a result, if there is an adult defendant who is responsible for the behaviour of under 18-year-olds, it may be better to issue in the adult court, particularly if the adult is also accused of ASB. In practice it is often more practical to apply for an injunction only

---

49 Part 1 of Schedule 2 of the Act

against an adult, provided that the proposed defendant is able to exercise some control over the juvenile.

7. In rare cases, there may be doubts as to the age of a defendant. Section 20 (2) provides that "*a person's age is treated for the purposes of this Part is being that which it appears to the court to be after considering any available evidence.*"

8. Therefore, even if a defendant produces an identity document showing that they are under the age of 18, if the court has evidence to the contrary before it, it can conclude that the proceedings should continue in the County Court rather than the youth court.

Applications in the Youth Court

9. If a decision has been taken to proceed in the Youth Court, it is mandatory (in paragraph 1.8 of the PAP) except in cases of real urgency when a without notice application is made, that before issuing the applicant should consult with the local youth offending team ("YOT") and any other bodies (e.g. social services, police/landlord/medical staff which it is thought appropriate.

10. There is conflict between the Act, which excuses cases of real urgency and the wording of the draft PAP, which asserts that consultation with the YOT "*must take place before the application is made*". Clearly, in some cases, an applicant would have reason to ignore the Protocol and issue the application, informing the YOT. If a decision is taken not to consult before issue, or even the making of the interim injunction, reasons should be given in the witness statement, and they should then be informed when appropriate.

11. It is for the applicant to decide who should be consulted, but care should be taken to justify in the witness statements any decision to exclude any particular body or person if they are already dealing with the young person.

12. If time is tight, it may still be possible to get the YOT to sit at short notice or for the consultation to take place remotely.[50]

13. Given the wording of the forthcoming PAP, if a decision not to consult has been taken and is later found to be wrong or unreasonable, it does not mean that the injunction should be refused or discharged.

14. The statutory test should be applied, and a balancing act undertaken. The applicant may have to argue that, while there was a breach of the duty to consult, the court should balance that breach by the applicant against the interests of the victims.

15. Those organisations can only give their view on the merits, they cannot prevent an application going ahead. When considering whether it is just convenient to the injunction, the defendant will no doubt press the court to refuse it on the basis that one of the agencies concerned does not feel that it is fair to the juvenile.

16. If the youth offending team is already involved with an under 18-year-old, their support is likely to be important, both in securing the injunction and in later efforts to ensure compliance.

17. An application for a power of arrest against a youth should only be made after consultation with the YOT, the result of which should be presented in the witness statement. Examples are given in the Practitioners Guide of cases where a POA might be appropriate.

18. Applications in respect of adults alone are made to the County Court, or in exceptional cases to the High Court, but if action has to be initiated against a mixture of over and under 18-year olds, the applicant can apply to the Youth Court for permission to add

---

[50] Youth Justice Board YOT Practitioners Guide to Civil Injunctions, which applicants should obviously use in the decision-making and planning stages of any application

the adult application(s) to the proceedings in that court.[51] This obviously saves the cost of two separate applications.

19. However, the Youth Court has to find that it is in the interests of justice to hear the applications against the under and over 18-year-olds together. Defendants are likely to apply to have the cases heard separately, for obvious reasons.

20. Once an injunction is granted, if the defendant is either 18 (and was dealt with in the Youth Court with a youth) or they turn 18, they will be dealt with in the adult court system.[52]

Care Leavers Aged 18 to 25

21. The Protocol also addresses cases where proceedings are brought against care leavers, requiring the applicant first to ascertain whether the respondent has a personal adviser (cf section 3 of the Children & Social Work Act 2017) and, if so, to consult. If the respondent does not have a personal adviser, the applicant should advise them as to their entitlement to have one (paragraph 1.9 of the draft Protocol).

Preparing the application

Statutory Guidance issued under s 19 of the Act

22. The Act allows the Secretary of State to issue guidance to those entitled to apply for injunctions. It is essential reading for both applicants and respondents. The "statutory guidance for front-line professionals" was revised in June 2022.[53] If that Guidance has not been followed, a defendant will have a good first line of attack

---

[51] Section 18 (2)

[52] Sections 8(2)(b), 9(3)(b) and 10(2)(b)

[53] Antisocial Behaviour, Crime and Policing Act 2014: Antisocial Behaviour Powers, Statutory Guidance for Frontline Professionals, June 2022 edition

against the grant of an injunction, particularly as it will be supported by the PAP.

Duty of full and frank disclosure

23. Those preparing the application and/or presenting it in court should remind themselves of the duty of full disclosure. This is particularly important on interim hearings, especially those without notice, where a failure to disclose can have disastrous consequences. But the duty of disclosure applies throughout an application and in committal proceedings.

24. Applications must be made (quoting from the excellent Nearly Legal blog) in a "*fair and even-handed manner, drawing attention to evidence and arguments that it can reasonably anticipate the absent party would wish to make.*" Note that:

    1. the applicant needs to include material both helpful and prejudicial to the applicant;

    2. the evidence must not have the effect of misleading the court, and must give the judge confidence in the thoroughness and objectivity of the application;

    3. it is up to a claimant to make proper enquiries before issuing the application, which includes investigating any defences available.

25. By way of example, in a case where the tenant has been resident for a long period but the ASB has only just started, it is essential to explain why it has suddenly begun and the reason injunctive proceedings are necessary in preference to some alternative method of control.

26. For a reminder of what might happen if the applicant does not disclose all relevant material to the court at the first hearing, see *Southern Housing Group Ltd v Stephen Berry*[54].

27. That was a case where the claimant knew of (1) the defendant's long history of illness and diagnosis of major depressive disorder, undertook a PSED assessment and (2) numerous serious counter-allegations, but did not tell the court at the first, without notice hearing.

28. In an application to discharge the injunction because of that non-disclosure, the Deputy District Judge found that the interim order should be discharged, which he said might potentially be a problem for the claimant but was not one of his main considerations.

29. The decision left the tenant victims, who were said to be "*fearful for their lives as a result of the death threats, racist and homophobic remarks*" which the judge described as "*some very disturbing allegations*", without any protection until the final hearing.

30. Thus, if material has been omitted from the witness statements by mistake, it is still possible (and indeed essential) to correct that omission, even at the interim hearing, by giving oral evidence or providing to the court further documents in disclosure. An apology to the court might be necessary, but this can be given by the advocate after explaining the importance and extent of the duty of full disclosure.

[54] County Court at Clerkenwell and Shoreditch, 25 February 2021, transcript available online. The court relied on the principles in *Tugushev v Orlov [2019] EWHC 2031*, decided on 26 July 2019.

Procedural requirements

31. Applicants also need (1) to be familiar with the CPR and the Practice Directions and (2) with the basic law and to anticipate what is likely to be raised by a defendant.

32. Procedural mistakes can lead to embarrassment and potentially to partial or total failure of the application. CPR 23 and CPR 25 and their Practice Directions need to be studied and understood. CPR 65.42-49 also adds specific Rules dealing with practice and procedure relating to ASBIs which must be read and followed.

Fees payable for injunction applications

33. The application is subject to the Part 8 procedure, as modified by CPR 65. Despite being issued under Part 8, the full issue fee is not payable. Applicants should resist any attempt by the court to extract the higher amount. The proper issue fee in 2022 is £332 as fixed by the Civil Proceedings Fees Order, Part 1C, Fee 1.5- "Any Other Remedy (County Court)" (effective March 2022), set out in the Civil and Family Court Fees form, EX50. In the High Court the fee Is £569.

34. Applications must be made on Form N16A, general form of application for interim injunction.[55] An example of an N16A appears in the Appendix. Some like to make them using "Particulars of Claim" although there is absolutely no need for such expensive measures and it is wrong in principle to use them.

35. If the application isn't made to the County Court which serves the address where the defendant lives or the conduct complained of occurred the court will transfer it to the relevant hearing centre.

[55] CPR PD 65.1 (1), which is treated as the Part 8 claim form

36. Applicants are specifically warned in the Practice Direction that they should consider the potential delay which may result if an application is not made at the appropriate hearing centre in the first instance.[56] This is particularly important for organisations whose head office is distant from the relevant court centre.

The witness statement(s)

37. One might think that an application can be made using the N16A form alone,[57] but CPR 65.43(2)(c) requires at least one witness statement to be filed. CPR 23.7 (3) (a) requires that an application notice must be accompanied by a copy of any witness statement made in support, although it is standard practice to file additional evidence after the first hearing.

38. Usually the first witness statement comes from an employee of the applicant, or a police officer. It sets out an overall picture of why the injunction is being sought.

Evidence as to compliance with the PAP

39. The statement must include details of what has been done in an attempt to avoid applying for an injunction.

40. When the PAP comes into force the provision of this information will become mandatory, as Part 3 says that the application "should" be accompanied by evidence on the eight requirements set out in paragraphs (a)-(h), which form a checklist of how the pre-action section of the statement should look:

(a) What steps have been taken to address any anti-social

---

56 CPR 65.1 (2)

57 CPR PD 23 A .9 .7 says that the contents of the application notice may be used as evidence except at a trial, as long as they have been verified by a statement of truth.

behaviour before seeking an order under the Act whether by an early intervention approach or alternative approach (e.g. mediation or restorative justice) or otherwise.

(b) *Confirmation that there has been compliance with the applicant's relevant internal policies (if any) and any local plan in relation to consultation before commencing action in relation to anti-social behaviour.*

(c) *Grounds for any belief that the respondent is, or may be, vulnerable and/or has mental health or capacity issues.*

(d) *Details of any difficulty the respondent may have in reading or understanding information and what steps have been taken in light of such difficulty.*

(e) *Details of the steps taken to advise the respondent as to how to obtain legal representation or any other assistance in respect of potential action.*

(f) *Details of consideration of the need/potential for positive requirements within the order.*

(g) *If the applicant seeks a power of arrest to any proposed term, an explanation of the basis by which the statutory test under section 4 is met.*

(h) *If the application is made without notice, the reasons why notice has not been given (see CPR 25.3(3)).*

41. Your main witness statement should run through these requirements at the outset, and if it involves a defendant between the ages of 10 and 25, the paragraphs 1.8 or 1.9 have been complied with as appropriate, and if not why.

42. If the applicant has good reason(s) not to comply with Part 2 of the PAP, the details should be included in the witness statement. Examples are given of the following:

- that the applicant considers it appropriate to take urgent action (i.e. a subjective test, satisfied by the deponent giving evidence that the issue was considered);

- when immediate action is necessary for the protection of any person (e.g. when telling a prospective defendant of the intended application would cause them to commit further harm to the victim);

- when the applicant has been asked not to contact the perpetrator by another agency and it considers that a reasonable request;

- when there has been an attempt to avoid legal action already in relation to previous complaints. This is likely to be the case in almost every situation, but an applicant should be aware that the defendant might subsequently argue that things have changed since they failed to cooperate and now they will comply with, e.g., a treatment order. Thus it pays to check with a defendant before issue of the application that they still refuse to cooperate.

43. Note that good reasons not to comply with the Protocol are not limited to the above, so it might also be appropriate to proceed without complying with Part 2 for other reasons, although the above four appear to provide explanations wide enough to cover most of the situations which an applicant will encounter.

44. If paragraphs of the Protocol 2.6-2.9 are not complied with, or complied with only in part, again the statement should explain why.

45. Paragraph 1.6 also provides that the court should take into account whether the PAP has been followed when considering whether to make an order, and, if so, its terms. In the event of any failure to comply with the Protocol there will be a specific power to impose sanctions (under paragraph 3.2) in the form of costs, adjournment, strike out or dismissal of the claim, but only if the court is satisfied (presumably on the submission of the defendant, on the balance of probabilities) that such failure was *unreasonable.*

46. The Cambridge Dictionary definition of "*not based on or using good judgment; not fair*" and the Oxford version "*not guided by all based on good sense*" give a good indication of what needs to be established.

47. An applicant who is found to have unreasonably failed to comply might also invite the court to consider (1) whether there is any prejudice to the defendant, and if so, (2) whether it can be addressed, either immediately by putting the hearing back for some time, or in any event, by the time of the next hearing.

48. It is difficult to conceive of a breach of the requirements which cannot be remedied swiftly. In an appropriate case (for instance a first hearing where there is an urgent need to impose an injunction but a particular body has not been consulted), the judge might make the order, on condition that the applicant consults by the return date.

49. As the Protocol expressly recognises in paragraph 1.3, "*applications made under ASB CPA 2014 are different to civil claims which solely involve the private rights and interests of the parties to the litigation as they are brought as part of the applicant's wider public protection functions*".

50. Thus the interests of victims is also relevant to the question whether the court should either amend the terms of any injunction, or make sanctions. Those public protection functions

should be at the forefront of the mind of the court in making any order.

51. Refusal of an injunction would leave victims of ASB unprotected and would only be appropriate in the most serious of breaches, for instance where those individuals themselves are at fault in such a way as to deprive them of the protection of the Act.

52. Given that such victims are likely to be at least distressed, if not traumatised, and so more prone e.g. to making errors or failing to attend court, the circumstances in which relief would be denied must be limited indeed.

53. Equally, when public bodies are pursuing legal claims purely for the protection of the public (or their employees etc), the court will lean against making a costs order in favour of a successful defendant, more so when they are publicly funded.

'Functional' elements of the statement

54. It will also deal with the individual allegations of antisocial behaviour, usually in chronological order. However, if a serious incident results in the need for an order, explanation of that 'trigger' event might come first in the statement, with subsequent coverage of the wider history. The content of witness statements is addressed in more detail below.

55. It is important that witness statements are prepared properly, in accordance with CPR 32.8 and the Practice Direction. The following are particularly important:

- para 17 on headings;
- para 18.1 the need to put the statement if practicable in the intended witness's own words, expressed in first person, stating full name and address, position held an occupation, then description of their role in the proceedings;

- para 18.2: they must state which of the facts set out our statements made from their own knowledge, and which are matters of information or belief and, if necessary, the source of any matters of that information or belief;

- para 18.3 identify the exhibits and verify them;

- para 18.4-6 ensure the exhibits are properly attached and numbered;

- ensure the size and quality of the paper, page and paragraph numbering, font size, and that the statement is in chronological order and that each subject is properly separated (use subheadings);

- para 20: make sure the statement of truth is properly done, signed and dated;

- para 23: filing witness statements properly is essential;

- para 26: in interim applications witness statement standards evidence and no live evidence is given. There is no need to bring the witnesses to court at the first hearing unless you have offered them the opportunity to see the inside of the court room and familiarise themselves.

56. The CPR are often ignored in the preparation of statements and this can annoy the tribunal. The Civil Court Practice warns "*There are many other extensive provisions contained in Practice Direction 32 and it is suggested that any practitioner preparing written evidence under the CPR should, until familiar with the provisions of PD 32, refer to it with care...*" You have been warned!

57. It is essential that the witness's own words be used as far as practicable and that nobody tries to persuade a witness what they

should say, or to bully or make or other inducements to them to put things a certain way.[58]

58. While it is important to prepare a good, chronological history of the circumstances in which you seek your injunction and give the court the facts it needs to find the tests satisfied, it's important not to end up with a statement which is unnecessarily long. Two major improvements can be made to most such statements:

- if referring to a sequence of ASB reported/experienced by more than one victim, give a chronological list of highly summarised incidents, with a reference to the relevant page number of the exhibit(s) in which the evidence of that incident appears;

- include a copy only of the relevant pages of any long documents, e.g. the front and signed pages of tenancy agreement, together with the 'nuisance' clause. Mention that the remainder of the document will be disclosed and then remember to do so.

59. Stick to the facts in a witness statement-do not use them, however tempting it might be, to advance arguments or to make innuendos. That said, if going through the history of a case it is necessary to explain why certain actions were taken, a certain amount of opinion is bound to be relevant.

60. For instance, an antisocial behaviour officer might consider the evidence and be of the opinion that one remedy is preferable to another. As the decision-making process which resulted in that course of action being chosen may be the subject of review, the opinion formed is relevant evidence.

---

[58] *Aquarius Financial Enterprises Inc v Certain Underwriters at Lloyd's* [2001] 2 Lloyd's rep 542

Deciding which incidents to include in the witness statement

61. The applicant can rely on incidents no matter how old they are in support of the claim. The six-month time period referred to in section 21 (7) of the Act does not restrict an applicant's choice of the timeframe to which it refers in its evidence.

62. An applicant needs only to prove that there has been qualifying behaviour after 23 September 2014. Then, even acts which occurred before that date can be relevant to the question of whether there has been ASB and whether it is just and convenient to grant an injunction.

63. Although the time limit is of little relevance any more given the passage of time since the Act came into force, some respondents will argue that events more than a few months previously should not be considered on either of the tests. This is obviously wrong-see judgement of Mr Justice Holroyde at paragraph 36 in *Birmingham City Council v Glenn Pardoe:*[59]

> "*On long established principles applicable in both civil and criminal contexts, past behaviour may be probative of more recent behaviour: for example, as similar fact evidence which is probative of the identity of the perpetrator of the recent conduct, or as evidence which serves to rebut a defensive accident or innocent error.*"

64. It is unlikely that in most cases behaviour dating from a number of years ago will be directly relevant to an application. However sometimes it is necessary to show a course of conduct, or to stress the long-term nature of the problem, particularly if there have been only a few incidents but past experience has shown that things can worsen they are allowed to progress.

---

[59] *Birmingham City Council v Glenn Pardoe* [2016] EWHC 3119 (QB)

Proving facts by inference

65. The judgement in *Birmingham v Pardoe*[60] also contains useful guidance on how to use evidence to establish that someone is responsible for ASB in cases where there is no direct evidence or where there may be a defence of 'innocent explanation':

> *"Suppose, for example, that a respondent had made his neighbours' lives a misery by a specific form of anti-social behaviour (say, graffiti of a particular kind) over a period of months prior to 23rd September 2014, but had then been imprisoned for unrelated matters at a time when the local authority was about to commence a claim for an injunction. Suppose that within days of his release from prison, graffiti of that particular kind suddenly reappeared, but there was only limited direct evidence available to prove that the perpetrator was the respondent rather than an unknown person with a coincidental penchant for such graffiti. It would to my mind be very surprising if Parliament had intended to prevent the authority from adducing any evidence about the previous incidents if it would otherwise be admissible in order to prove the identity of the perpetrator. In the same way, if a respondent repeatedly caused a nuisance by holding noisy parties late at night, but claimed that the occasions when that had happened after 23rd September 2014 had occurred without any fault on his part when unknown persons had unexpectedly gate-crashed his parties, it would be very surprising if Parliament had intended to prevent the authority from adducing any evidence about the earlier parties if it was otherwise admissible in order to rebut that defence."*

66. There are two points useful in practice:

---

60 (again at para 36)

- first one can prove that a respondent is likely to have behaved in a certain way by showing a pattern from which the court can infer culpability, together with opportunity and motive, without any direct evidence linking the defendant to the incident;

- second, evidence going back into the mists of time can prevent a respondent from relying on a defence of 'accident' or other innocent explanation.

67. In general, is better to include in the application information which may only seem the time to be of limited relevance, than to leave it out and later be accused of being selective or be unable to meet a defence which could have been disproved had the earlier allegations or evidence been included.

68. Every case will be different, in that some defendants challenge everything, while others accept the content of witness statements on their face. Although it is a gross generalisation, defendant to a more experienced in the criminal courts and have many previous convictions tend to challenge every factual assertion. They are inclined to deny everything unless there is first-hand evidence, mistakenly believing that the court cannot take into account hearsay.

69. If possible, it is helpful to consider what a defendant might say in answer to the application and to address it before it is said. If a defence isn't anticipated, it may succeed where it should not do so. Counter-allegations, excuses and reasons for apparent ASB should be considered. The possibility of Equality Act issues needs to be investigated, and with more rigour on the coming into force of the Protocol.

Addressing disability/capacity issues at an early stage

70. If a review of any decision is relevant, the arguments raised by both sides must be included in the statement. This is particularly so in discussing any Equality Act 2010/disability issues and questions of capacity under the Mental Capacity Act 2005. Care needs to be taken to follow any protocol or policy for defendants who are or may be disabled, particularly by mental illness.[61] If the claimant thinks the defendant may lack capacity, the appropriate steps must be followed to protect his interests. Once the Protocol comes into force, these steps will be as good as mandatory, except in very urgent cases.

71. Perpetrators can see themselves as (and sometimes are) victims, or can be subject to revenge attacks, as well as in some cases being unable to prevent the behaviour concerned. Conditions such as ADHD, Asperger's syndrome, schizophrenia, autism, brain injuries and obsessive-compulsive disorder can give rise to alarming or violent behaviours. A defendant may be able to show that the behaviour has happened "because of something arising in consequence of the disability".

72. The court will not make an order against a respondent who lacks capacity to comply with its terms. If there are issues as to a defendant's ability to understand the injunction, care must be taken to adduce evidence of their ability to comply with court orders. Medical evidence as to lack of capacity may not satisfy a judge that the defendant did not have capacity to carry out the acts alleged against him. A court may decide to make an order against a defendant in the face of such evidence if it does not address the issues fully.[62]

---

61 familiarity with *Akerman-Livingstone v Aster Communities Ltd (formerly Flourish Homes Ltd)* [2015] UKSC 15 is essential

62 *Evesham & Pershore Housing Association v Werrett* [2015] EWHC 1060

73. The Court of Appeal has said that a mere likelihood that a defendant is disabled is not enough-there has to be evidence of the existence of a disability.[63] That was a case where the District Judge was said to have "*become a self-appointed medical expert by e.g. relying on his own medical dictionary to fill in the gaps*" as the medical evidence before the court did not establish the existence of Asperger's syndrome. In evidence the defendant himself had denied that his condition had an effect with anything other than how he 'integrated with society'.

74. Even if the disability causes the behaviour complained of, the court does not have to dismiss an application for an injunction just because the causal link is established.

75. Behaviour arising from alcohol or drug addiction is not protected by the Equality Act.[64]The court may conclude that the mental illness is caused by voluntary drug taking or alcohol consumption rather than an underlying mental health condition and is not protected by the 2010 Act.[65]

76. Alternatively, it may find that although the behaviour is only partially caused by drugs or alcohol and partly by a protected disability, it is still appropriate to make an order.

77. Further, even if a defendant is disabled, it may still be appropriate to make the order, if the imposition of an injunction is considered by the court to be a proportionate means of achieving a legitimate

---

(QB)

63 *Swan Housing Association Ltd v Cary Gill* [2013] EWCA Civ 1566

64 see for example how *Akerman-Livingstone* was applied in E*ales v Havering LBC* [2018] EWHC 2423 (QB) noted on Nearly Legal and transcript in Lawtel

65 see for instance: *R (on the application of Baisden v Leicester City Council* [2011] EWHC 3219 (Admin)

aim. Bringing injunctive proceedings against people suffering from disabilities is usually considered a last resort.

78. Accordingly in many cases, the injunction will be the only thing, short of eviction, which will protect members of the public from an individual's behaviour. Additionally, if the injunction contains positive requirements on the defendant to obtain treatment, it may prove to be beneficial to both parties.

79. It is also necessary to consider whether a perpetrator might themselves be a victim, for instance in a case of 'cuckooing', where a defendant is targeted by a drugs gang and is so intimidated that they cannot prevent the gang from using their premises. In those circumstances, consideration should be given to bringing proceedings against the gang members as well as or instead of the tenant.

80. Treatment of disability defences is a matter for careful analysis and preparation, and the approach of the court is a structured investigation[66] beyond the scope of this guide.[67]

81. A study of any historic files and medical records may be necessary to ascertain whether a claim of disability is genuine. When disability is raised as a defence, the defendant should be asked to disclose their medical records so far as they are relevant. In choosing a Single Joint Expert it is helpful to instruct a doctor who has written reports for both sides. When the Protocol comes into force respondents will argue that the exclusions from protection of the Equality Act do not prevent the court from taking into account those conditions, given the requirement to investigate vulnerabilities without restriction.

---

[66] see the checklist in *Bracking v SSWP* (2013) EWCA Civ 1345, at para 26

[67] see for instance *Powell v Dacorum BC [*2019*]* EWCA Civ 23 and *Forward v Aldwyck Housing Group Ltd* [2019] EWHC 24 (QB)

82. It may be necessary for a claimant to obtain its own medical evidence, using an agency to instruct an independent doctor to look at the medical records and possibly even assess the defendant in person. One particular medical report agency has come in for significant criticism because their doctors have not been able to interview the had to work from a review of the medical records and the defendant's report.

83. Even if the applicant is unable to file and serve the resulting report in such circumstances, it often provides invaluable information for the purposes of questions or cross-examination of the defendant's doctor who may have been instructed on the basis of information which is more favourable to the defendant.

84. Once a disability defence has been raised and fully considered by the court, unless there has been a change of circumstance a defendant cannot then attempt to avoid the consequences of proceedings against him by asking the court to reconsider the impact of the disability at a later stage.[68]

85. Defendants often raise disability issues in circumstances where the claimant is taken by surprise, for instance because they allege mental illness which was not mentioned on a housing application form and/or had not manifested itself in any interaction with the defendant.

86. In cases where the applicant was unaware of a disability, or other vulnerability, a defendant raising such a defence at the eleventh hour may find themselves unable fully to rely on it. In *Taylor v Slough Borough Council*[69] the High Court judge said, (on appeal against the making of a possession order):

[68] *Paragon Homes Ltd v Neville* [2018] EWCA Civ 1712

[69] (2020) EWHC 3520 (Ch)

The duty to "have due regard" will then only take on any substance when the disability becomes or ought to have become apparent. In such cases, the lateness of the knowledge may impact on the discharge of the PSED. For example, cases may arise in which countervailing interests justify a less formal PSED assessment than would otherwise have been appropriate. Thus a tenant whose anti-social conduct has already been adversely affecting his neighbours for a considerable time but whose disability is raised at the eleventh hour may well find that the discharge of the PSED does not necessarily mandate a postponement of the date or enforcement of a possession order. Of course, the obligation to have "due regard" still arises but the result of the discharge of that obligation may well be less favourable to the person affected where, through delay, the landlord's options have been limited and the rights and reasonable expectations of others have assumed a more pressing character. Each case will, of course, depend on its own facts.

87. This principle applies equally in injunction applications, although the Protocol will necessitate consideration of the potential for disability etc at an early stage. The *Taylor* case is essential reading for anyone concerned with claims against tenants who may or do have a disability. It provides a helpful summary of the law and guidance as to how to comply with the PSED.

'Tidying up' the witness statement

88. At the end of the statement, it is necessary to summarise the content briefly, and to state why the particular relief is being sought. That is to say the reason for going without notice, reasons for including various paragraphs in the draft injunction and the justification for asking for a power of arrest on any of those clauses, individually.

89. If a witness statement contains inadmissible evidence or is otherwise in breach of CPR 32.4 (1), a party can apply to strike out the inadmissible parts of it.

90. Simply serving a witness statement is obviously not enough to get that evidence admitted-if you wish to rely on it at trial (rather than just at interim hearings) you must either (1) call the witness to give oral evidence, or (2) adduce it as hearsay evidence using the 1995 Act and CPR 33.2 or 33.3, serving notice if necessary.

91. But even if notice has not been served of intention to rely on hearsay evidence, the court can still be asked to consider it. This is an invaluable and underused power, as many people seem to believe that hearsay evidence is not admissible in the civil courts, or that if a witness refuses to come to court, there evidence cannot be used.

92. In the period between issue of the claim and the first hearing, there is often further nuisance. Is essential to provide the court with admissible evidence of all allegations. Further witness statements should be added to the bundle, filed and served as necessary and the index adjusted.

Interpretation: section 20-physical and mental injury

93. This section contains an important definition, and it is often necessary to remind the court of the content, preferably in the evidence. It says that "harm" includes "*serious ill-treatment or abuse, whether physical or not*".

94. Some judges do not appreciate that a power of arrest can be granted when there is no risk of physical violence and there are no threats. The only threshold according to the statute is that *serious abuse or ill-treatment* must have occurred, which may not *yet* have led to any physical or mental damage.

95. Care must be taken when pursuing the grant of the power of arrest on interim, ex-parte applications (see below). While it may seem a sensible idea at the time, it is necessary to consider carefully what evidence there is to support the application and explicitly to point

that out to the court. If this is done in writing, the defendant will be able to understand how the decision was made to impose it.

CHAPTER SIX
PROHIBITIONS AND REQUIREMENTS

KEY POINTS

1. ASB Injunctions can include both negative and positive terms
2. Negative/prohibitory terms
3. Exclusion orders
4. Positive/mandatory requirements
5. Duration of injunction orders
6. Powers of arrest
7. Applying for a warrant where there is no power of arrest

Introduction

1. Traditionally injunctions have always been more readily granted to prevent people from doing acts ("a prohibitory injunction") rather than being positive orders requiring the respondent to do something ("mandatory" orders). The courts have always said that it should be more difficult to obtain a mandatory injunction than a prohibitory one.

ASB Injunctions can now include both negative and positive terms

2. The 2014 Act introduced the concept of terms both prohibiting behaviour and those requiring defendants to participate in activities which might reduce or prevent ASB.

3. Terms of an injunction should be clear, so that the respondent can understand what they must or must not do. This is particularly so if there is any restriction on activities which would otherwise be lawful, or in respect of exclusion orders.

Negative/prohibitory terms

4. The Guidelines provide examples of the sort of terms which might be used. A list of behaviours which the defendant exhibits forms the basis of the terms sought. They should be analysed to formulate terms which prevent the 'building blocks' of the ASB.

5. Negative terms are an altogether easier concept than positive requirements. The most obvious and frequently used are those preventing:

    - conduct which causes or is likely to cause a nuisance or annoyance or constitutes harassment;
    - the use of abusive or threatening words or behaviour;
    - the threat or use of violence;
    - the use and distribution of drugs;
    - contact with certain individuals or witnesses;
    - access to a property, an area or to the defendant's own home.

6. More creative prohibitions target behaviour which leads to or is an essential precondition of antisocial behaviour, for instance leaving home at certain times, going to a particular area or building, carrying or being in possession of certain items e.g. tools or weapons, aerosol paint or alcohol.

7. An alcoholic defendant might be prevented from buying alcohol in or from entering certain shops in the locality, as well as drinking in public places. A term can be imposed prohibiting any drinking in public or exceptionally, possessing or drinking any alcohol at all, or storing alcohol in the home, against driving certain types of vehicle, or associating with named or individuals or people specified by a description.

8. Terms in the injunction must be precise and capable of being understood by the defendant and any breach should be readily identifiable and capable of being proved.[70]

9. When formulating terms for an injunction it is a challenge to look at proposed terms objectively from the point of view of the court studying them at the enforcement stage. At this point a defendant will be keen to point to any ambiguity or lack of clarity. The rule is that orders should be interpreted against the party who drafted them. If there are two possible interpretations, that most favourable to a defendant should be given to a term.

Exclusion orders

10. When a social housing landlord, a local authority or the police apply for the injunction, they can exceptionally ask for an order excluding a defendant aged 18 or over from any address where they normally live, including their own home.

---

[70] *R v Boness & others* [2005] EWCA Crim 2395

11. In this context housing providers are only those who have a lease of more than three years, so some short-term social housing accommodation will not be within the section.[71] This is important to bear in mind if the housing provider has taken a short-term lease of accommodation for, e.g., homelessness reduction. In that case the local authority or police might ask for an Injunction.

12. Also, registered providers cannot ask for an exclusion order in respect of a privately-owned home in the middle of one of their estates – again they need to get the police or local authority to apply. If the home is privately rented, they need to consult the landlord. This is obviously a step which is likely to have been taken already, as persuading a landlord to evict an antisocial tenant saves resources.

13. The claimant must be able to adduce evidence either that there have been threats or actual violence, or that there is a significant risk of harm from the defendant to other people.[72] The wording of the section means that an individual cannot be excluded if they have professed an intention to self-harm in the property.

14. The applicant need only persuade the court to "think" that the respondent will cause harm to others.[73] Some judges believe that the test is that there has been violence or threats *and* that there is a significant risk of harm. Although this is not how the Act is worded, it arises out of something said in *Moat Housing* – and relates to hearings without notice, when the court said that this was the relevant test. It is important to remind the court of the restriction on its power if this is an issue.

---

[71] Section 13 (2) (b)

[72] section 13 (1) (c) (i) and (ii)

[73] Section 13 (1) (c)

15. The same applies to the imposition of a power of arrest. Regrettably, neither of these restrictions on the grant of such relief appears in the statute and both of them can provide a real handicap to obtaining relief for victims on ex-parte applications.

16. For this reason, in cases of any severity or urgency, if the court refuses to grant a power of arrest or exclusion in a case in which the applicant believes it essential, an applicant should ensure that the return date is listed within a very short period of time-a matter of days. If in the meantime there is a breach, an ex-parte application can be made for a warrant of arrest.

17. When the police or a local authority make such an application, they can ask for the order to apply for any property, whether they own or manage it, whereas other social landlords are limited to properties within their ownership or control.

Positive/mandatory requirements

18. The 2014 Act introduced the concept of positive requirements in ASBIs.[74] In practice they have not proved very popular. Negative terms remain the usual format of most orders.

19. The Court of Appeal has lamented that positive requirements are rarely used in the civil courts "because the institutional framework necessary to allow them to be made is absent."[75] No doubt the primary issue is the absence of the availability of funding, and the pressure on the public purse from other quarters.

20. Positive requirements have traditionally been a recognised part of injunctive law. They are described as "mandatory" terms of the

---

[74] section 1 (3)

[75] in *Christopher Lovett v Wigan Borough Council* and others [2022] EWCA Civ 1631

order. They might be a positive way of expressing a negative, e.g. to stay out of a particular area, or a requirement to do something, e.g. a term requiring a defendant to surrender all knives or other offensive weapons in his possession and to permit the claimant to enter his property and to search it to confirm that he has done so. That type of term is nearly always possible to phrase either positively or negatively.

True 'positive requirements'

21. Positive requirements were intended to help to prevent future ASB by dealing with the underlying causes of poor behaviour, e.g. requiring a defendant to undergo drug or alcohol treatment, improving attendance at school or other training, reporting to the police at regular times or taking a dog to behavioural training classes.

22. Unfortunately, such positive requirements must be accompanied by specification of an individual or organisation responsible for ensuring compliance by the respondent with the requirements. That supervision might be provided by the addiction or counselling service, or by the youth offending team etc.

23. The supervisor must make the necessary arrangements for the requirements to be fulfilled, promote compliance with them, and keep the applicant and the police updated as to compliance or breach[76]. In practice it has proved a challenge to find the finance for positive requirements and to find individuals or organisations who are willing to set aside time not just to supervise, but to report back to the court.

---

[76] Section 3 (4)

24. Also, when proposing a requirement, evidence has to be provided about its suitability and enforceability from the person or organisation charged with supervision.[77]

25. If the court is thinking of imposing more than one requirement, it must consider specifically whether each is compatible with the other,[78] creating another hoop through which the claimant must jump to obtain an order. It is easy to acknowledge that as a concept, but more difficult to remember to ensure that the court records that it has considered the question in its judgement, or better, in the preamble to the order.

26. The Act does not say who has to fund the positive requirements. Obviously, most respondents will not have sufficient financial resources and the bill has to be paid by the applicant, or any other body which can be persuaded to incur the expense.

27. The Act also specifies two additional requirements of every mandatory injunction which can be enforced as terms of the order-the respondent has to keep in touch with the supervisor and to notify them of any change of address.[79]

28. Often, prior to making an application for an injunction, the applicant will have attempted to work with the individual but they habitually refuse help repeatedly. If no action is taken against them during this time, victims of antisocial behaviour remain unprotected, which is clearly not desirable.

29. Given the apparent shift in emphasis evident from the CJC report towards a focus on the defendants rather than the victims, it would seem sensible to consider injunctive proceedings at an earlier stage. Then defendants can be required to accept help or

[77] Section 3 (2)

[78] Section 3 (3)

[79] Section 3 (6)

otherwise to face committal proceedings, thus providing relief for victims.

Duration of injunction orders

30. Although there is no minimum term, it is unusual to see an injunction requested or imposed for less than a year. Often behaviour is of such a long-standing nature that a two-year period is imposed, but longer orders can be justified on the evidence. Occasionally it is appropriate to ask for an indefinite order.

31. Courts and even individual judges tend to develop their own practice as to the duration of an order and it is sensible to provide evidence to justify any particular duration sought.

32. Factors affecting the duration of order sought will include the length of time that a defendant has been causing problems, whether there is any long-term addiction or personality issue, the identity of victims, the frequency of the defendant's contact with them and the prevalence of the issue in the locality.

Powers of arrest

33. As the application is being prepared, consideration should be given to which (if any) of the clauses the applicant will seek to attach a power of arrest under section 4 of the Act and CPR 65.44. If the conduct of a defendant is poor enough to be worth seeking an injunction, it will usually merit the imposition of a power of arrest on one or more of the terms.

34. Provided the test is met, a power of arrest can be attached to any term of an injunction (except a requirement to participate in an activity) and it should be borne in mind that without a power of arrest injunctions are significantly more difficult to enforce. Instead of being able to ask the police to arrest, either the applicant will have to apply for a warrant of arrest, or they will

need to make an application to commit the defendant. Both of these processes are addressed later in the book.

35. An applicant can ask for a power of arrest to be attached to *any* term of an injunction if the court believes that the defendant has used or threatened violence against another when they behaving in an antisocial manner *or* there is a risk of significant harm by them towards others. As framed in the Act, this is a wide test and deliberately so.

36. Subsequent case law has attempted to limit the imposition of powers of arrest to more restricted circumstances, but it is often necessary to ask for a power of arrest in respect of terms of the injunction which do not themselves necessarily lead to a risk of significant harm but are a necessary precursor, e.g. entering an area or the prohibition of acts likely to cause a nuisance or annoyance. It is better to ask for the power of arrest and be refused than to fail to try and then discover that it is difficult to enforce the injunction.

37. Where a term involves a certain degree of subjective analysis, e.g. "nuisance or annoyance" it may be more difficult to persuade the court to attach a power of arrest. Courts look favourably upon terms which are both easily understood and where it is clear that certain behaviour is objectively a breach.

38. Requests for powers of arrest must be based on what evidence is available to support that application. There is nothing to be gained from making an application with a number of terms and providing a draft power of arrest in respect of all of them without separate consideration. This may give the court the impression that insufficient thought has gone into the drafting of the application.

39. A power of arrest cannot be made in respect of a positive requirement to participate in an activity (e.g. attend a

rehabilitation unit).[80] It is therefore particularly important to word injunctions carefully, to avoid a defendant arguing that a requirement has the *effect* of making a defendant participate in a particular activity.

40. When a power of arrest is attached to any provision of an injunction, the claimant must deliver a copy of the relevant provisions to any police station for the area where the conduct occurred. if the injunction is granted without notice, a copy of the order must not be served on the police before has been served on the defendant.[81]

41. The court may make a power of arrest effective for a shorter period of time.[82] There is an obvious risk in doing so, because it is wise to keep injunction orders as simple as possible and a discrepancy between the two dates provides an ideal opportunity for a mistake to be made.

42. If a power of arrest has been validly attached, a police officer does not need a warrant to arrest for breach of a prohibition or a requirement of the injunction.[83]

43. If an order is subsequently varied or any provision discharged, the applicant must immediately inform the police station to which a copy of the injunction was delivered and subsequently deliver a copy of the new order to that station.[84]

---

80 Section 4 (1)

81 CPR 65.44 (2) (b) and (c)

82 Section 4(2)

83 Section 9 (1)

84 CPR 65.44 (4)

Applying for a warrant where there is no power of arrest

44. A decision may be taken not to apply for a power of arrest in respect of any particular term, or the court may refuse to attach one to a term of the injunction. This is not necessarily detrimental to the enforcement of the order, because upon breach the applicant can subsequently apply to the court for a warrant for the arrest of the defendant.

45. An application without notice can be made for such a warrant in respect of a breach of any term of the order to which a power of arrest could have been attached.[85] Making the application for the warrant is addressed separately in Chapter Twelve.

---

[85] Section 10 and CPR 65.49

CHAPTER SEVEN
INTERIM INJUNCTIONS

KEY POINTS

1. The power to make an interim injunction
2. Conditions for the grant of an interim order
3. Getting the procedure right
4. Draft orders
5. What needs to be filed and served?
6. Level of judge
7. Requesting a reasonable hearing time when filing
8. Listing the application
9. Serving a defendant with an on-notice application
10. Case summary, bundles and schedules
11. Preparing a Statement of Costs

The power to make an interim injunction

1. In almost every case, if the antisocial behaviour concerned behaviour is serious enough to merit seeking an injunction, the victims will need to be protected from the defendant fairly swiftly. This does not happen automatically upon issue of the

claim. Instead, when the application is first before the court, the claimant can ask for an interim injunction under the power provided in the Act.[86]

2. The application can be made with or without notice to the defendant. Without notice applications impose additional burdens on an applicant. Those extra duties are addressed in the next Chapter.

Conditions for the grant of an interim order

3. On the first occasion the application is put before the court, if it is not granted immediately, the court has a wide discretion to impose an interim injunction-section 7 (2) merely says that "*the court may grant an injunction*" under section 1) lasting until the final hearing or until further order if it "*thinks it just to do so*". Two points, discussed below, are important to note from the section itself:

   - an application for an interim injunction *should* only request an order which will last until the date fixed for a final hearing or 'further order' rather than the date sought for the final order, which may be years in advance;

   - the court does not have to be satisfied on the evidence that antisocial behaviour is *proved*-it only needs to be satisfied that it is just to grant an interim injunction.

Getting the procedure right

4. There is a Practice Direction specifically concerning interim injunctions-PD 25A, which supplements CPR 25. As almost every word of it is crucial to any application for an interim

86 Section 7

injunction, it is essential to read it and to follow every requirement.

5. A few points not generally recognised emerge:

   - as stated above, evidence in support can in rare cases be provided just on the notice of application;[87]
   - applications can be made when a claim form has not been issued;[88]
   - they can be dealt with in cases of extreme urgency by telephone;[89]
   - if made before the issue of a claim, unless the court orders otherwise the applicant must undertake to the court to issue a claim immediately for the court will give directions for starting the claim.[90]

6. Courts tend to be overworked and under resourced, so making life easier for court staff and judges is essential to avert avoidable adverse experiences. During preparation of papers for the hearing it is sensible to ask someone else to review everything to check that the correct forms have been used and the witness statements properly laid out, with page numbered exhibits etc.

---

[87] CPR PD 25 A .3 .2 (3)

[88] CPR 25.2 (1) (a) and CPR PD 25A .4 .1 (2)

[89] ibid, para 4.2

[90] CPR PD 25A.4.4 (1)-C also the rest of para 4.4 and 4.5 if making urgent applications

Draft orders

7. At the same time as preparing the application, a draft injunction order and power of arrest should be prepared, which should (obviously) reflect the contents of the N16A. Often the order will need to be explained by a plan, which shows the extent of the area relevant to the clauses of the injunction, so that a defendant can know for sure the extent of exclusion zone or the area over which certain conduct is prohibited.

8. The draft of any order needs to be provided electronically to the court, so that if the judge or the court staff wish to produce the order on the court service software, they will have the material content readily to hand. This also helps to reduce typographical errors in the drafting of orders which are otherwise regrettably common.

9. The N16 Injunction Order[91] form includes the words "(*whether by himself or by instructing or encouraging or permitting any other person*) …". It is important to check that the wording is correct. Provided this form is used, there should be no issue with a defendant's breach of injunction, assuming that they can be shown to have allowed the behaviour to happen or continue.

10. Undertakings are different, because the standard form contains no introductory wording.

11. Care must be taken: In a 2009 Court of Appeal decision[92], the perils of failing to word the undertaking properly were highlighted. The claimant had accepted a version which only said

---

[91] which can be found on the government Forms website

[92] *Circle 33 Housing Trust Limited v Kathirkmanathan* [2009] EWCA Civ 921, (2009) CA (Civ Div) 16/7/2009

"not to engage, or encourage others to engage, in conduct capable of causing a nuisance or noise".

12. This was particularly unfortunate on the facts of the case, when it is clear that most of the nuisance complained of was being caused by members of the defendant's family. The family had caused serious nuisance to neighbours, but there was no evidence that the defendant had either caused the noise himself or had encouraged it. The defendant's appeal against the County Court judge's findings of breach was allowed and he did not have to serve the sentence which had been imposed.

What needs to be filed and served?

13. The applicant needs to provide the court with a copy of bundles containing the N16A against each defendant, all evidence and exhibits in support, a draft order and power of arrest and plans, with additional copies for the court and the applicant. Good quality colour copies of any exhibits, photographs and plans are essential, both in the defendant's and in the court's bundles.

Level of judge

14. The applicant should ask that the application is listed before a District Judge, because the rules specifically state that they should normally hear these applications.[93] However some County Court list such applications before County Court Judges or Recorders. The route of appeal is different, so if possible, it is advisable to have them listed in front of a District Judge in the first instance.

Requesting a reasonable hearing time when filing

15. Courts usually list interim applications for anything between 10 and 30 minutes depending on the court centre. The N16A does

---

93 (Practice Direction 2B—Allocation of Cases to Levels of Judiciary para. 8.1 (v))

not have provision to give the court a time estimate. It is advisable to tell the court listing officer how long is needed in the letter/email accompanying the claim documents.

Listing the application

16. In practice, if the application is made on notice to the defendant, courts often take some time to issue the claim and then list the first hearing of an application weeks after it is issued. This was clearly not the intention of Parliament as reflected in the drafting of the Act. Efforts can be made to get a County Court listing within a short time after issue, possibly by writing a letter explaining why no application is made without notice, but an early date for the first hearing is sought.

17. The court will issue the application and return sealed copies for service, which must be personally effected for on-notice applications.[94] The rules specifically provide that the application can be listed for hearing before the expiry of the time a defendant is usually given to file an acknowledgement of service.

18. When the Notice of Hearing is received from the court, it is important to check that the correct time has been allowed. If too short a time has been allocated and there are voluminous papers, the court is unlikely to extend it.

19. Since the pandemic more cases have been dealt with remotely, by telephone or video hearings. This remains a reasonable approach, particularly for applications without notice. A request can be made at the time of filing the application.

---

94 CPR 65.43 (5)

20. However, when the defendant is notified, it is unusual now to allow the application to proceed remotely, despite the clear benefits to all except the court.

21. Obviously, in committal applications where the defendant is in custody, the police may ask that the remand hearing is remote, and they have facilities to allow for video hearings.

Serving a defendant with an on-notice application

22. The court expects the applicant to serve the papers on the defendant, which can either be done by a process server or by an employee of the claimant. The defendant must be served with the notice of issue and notice of hearing, along with stamped copies of the application papers.

23. On a hearing with notice, it is necessary to serve the defendant personally, as soon as practicable after issue,[95] unless the court otherwise directs, and in any event at least two days before the hearing.[96] Defendants can take part in the hearing whether or not they have filed an acknowledgement of service.

24. Personal service is achieved by leaving the documents with an individual.[97] They must be made aware of the contents and be given an opportunity to take them. If they subsequently refused to do so, or throw them away, it does not affect the validity of the service of those documents.

25. If there is insufficient time to serve, the applicant should give formal notice of the application unless circumstances require

---

96 CPR PD 23A para 4.1

97 CPR 65.43 (6) (a)

95 CPR 6.5 (3) (a)

secrecy, when the application becomes 'ex parte' and additional rules apply.[98]

Service by an alternative means

26. If a defendant evades service, an application should be made for service by an alternative means or at an alternative place under CPR 6.15 and 6.27. Such applications need to be made following the rules,[99] with evidence stating the reason why the order is sought what alternative method or places proposed and why the applicant believes that the document is likely to reach the person to be served by the method or at the place proposed.

27. An application can also be made under CPR 6.15 (2) and CPR 6.27that steps already taken to bring the claim form to the attention of a defendant by an alternative method or at an alternative place is good service, For obvious reasons they are usually made without notice. Any order made must specify the method or place of service, the date on which the claim form has been deemed served.

28. If a defendant is being particularly difficult about service, innovative means may be employed, including service by text message.[100] Other methods might involve the use of social media, sending of an email to a defendant, notification through members of the family or household (not children) or the attachment of the order to the front door of premises known to be occupied by a defendant. Service can be dispensed with under CPR 6.28.

---

[98] ibid, para 4.2

[99] cf CPR PD 6A

[100] *NPV v QEL [2018]* EWHC 703 (QB), which was a harassment case but can be relied upon

Certificate of service

29. The process server must provide a Certificate of Service, proving that the defendant has been served with the papers either personally or in accordance with an order for service by alternative means. It helps to include details of what was said on service etc., and confirmation that the defendant understood the terms of the order if possible.

30. It should be filed at court, preferably before the hearing, and the original brought along to court on the day of the hearing.

31. If the defendant does not turn up, or turns up and denies they have been served with any papers and service cannot be proved, the hearing cannot proceed. The application must either be adjourned or dismissed, unless the applicant can persuade the court to deal with the application on a 'without-notice' basis.

Case summary, bundles and schedules

32. In any but the simplest application, it is helpful to include with the papers a case summary, or at least details of the circumstances in which the relief is claimed, so the judge knows what evidence they are looking for before they open the papers.

33. Some judges require a separate schedule of incidents relied on in support of an application for a power of arrest. It is good practice to provide one in every case. Ideally, the schedule should set out where the evidence is to be found, by reference to witness name, page and paragraph number, with an exhibit page number.

34. The bundle should follow a logical order. It will contain all the documents prepared and served which are relevant to the application: N16A, draft N16 order and POA, colour plan(s) with outlining, witness statements with their exhibits and certificates of service. If there are more than a few documents,

dividers should be used to separate them. A paginated index should list the contents, divided by document type.

35. It is necessary to prepare at least four copies of the bundle: for the advocate, the court, the respondent and the witness box. It is worth printing a fifth copy in case the court cannot find the paper version filed or the defendant fails to bring theirs to court. There are independent companies which will paginate and print bundles for a modest fee. Colour copies of any plans and photographs can be added separately.

36. The CPR allow the court to grant an interim remedy whether or not there has been a claim for a final remedy of that kind.[101] This provision can be useful if the facts change after an application has been made and additional terms on an injunction become relevant. The 2014 Act expressly provides for variation of injunctions (see Chapter Fifteen).

37. On the night before the hearing, a further check with victims should be made to ensure that they have reported incidents to date. They should be reminded to contact the claimant immediately if anything happens on the eve of the hearing or overnight. Such evidence can be invaluable.

Preparing a Statement of Costs

38. The applicant can recover its costs, both in respect of legal fees and 'disbursements'. However, most Defendants will be unable to pay any costs order in full and they may be on legal aid.[102] If the applicant is using lawyers and an attempt is to be made to

---

[101] CPR 25.1 (4)

[102] which is available in some cases to contest the grant of an injunction and always in committals

recover costs, a Statement of Costs[103] should be prepared, filed and served at least 24-hours before the hearing.

39. If the defendant is on benefits, the court can still carry out an assessment of their means and make an order that they contribute towards the costs at the benefit deduction rate, which is currently about £3.40 per week. Such orders are rarely made. Although it may not make much of a dent in the legal bill, it can provide a deterrent and will remind defendants that there can be a cost to contesting proceedings unreasonably.

[103] which can be found at form N260 on the Forms website

CHAPTER EIGHT
INTERIM HEARINGS

KEY POINTS

1. The interim hearing

2. Standard of proof for interim hearings and the balance of convenience

3. Terms of the order

4. Duration of the interim order

5. Undertakings for damages

6. Directions

7. Preparing a draft of the order

8. Service of the order

The interim hearing

1. Some applicants attend the hearing themselves, appearing by their officers[104] if the claim is housing related.

2. Although the hearing will be listed for a particular time, the applicant should attend at court well before the listed hour.

---

[104] Though they might be wary appearing against qualified or competent opponents – see "Giles Peaker's Nearly Legal on 30.1.17 at 10:04 am

Having signed in with the court usher, it is rare to find a defendant at court early, but members of the applicant team should be able to find a room and run through last-minute administrative issues.

3. Remote hearings allow parties to save substantial amounts of time compared with an attended hearing, though the defendant will not usually be able to speak to the applicant just before the hearing. For this reason, if they have not yet arranged legal representation, it is sensible to visit the respondent on the day before or of the hearing if it is listed remotely.

4. The court will often have limited time available even when a hearing has been listed on notice, because courts are often over listed. Sometimes the judge will have read the papers, otherwise they will need a succinct summary of the reasons the injunction is sought, the rationale for the terms requested and the justification for any request for a power of arrest or exclusion.

5. The advocate should be able to identify the constituent elements necessary to establish their case by reference to the evidence supporting the allegations made. In a case of any complexity, a Scott Schedule is essential (see Chapter Three).

6. An interim application can proceed in many different ways: sometimes the defendant does not appear despite being served, sometimes they appear and are represented and occasionally they bring a 'McKenzie friend' in the hope that someone else can talk on their behalf. The court is unlikely to allow an unqualified individual to do more than give advice to a defendant.

7. Some judges prefer an opening and an explanation in writing of why the interim injunction sought. Others will have read the papers, formed their own view and either grant the injunction without further enquiry, or grant it in an amended form or refuse it on an interim basis. The court's power to dismiss an application

at the interim hearing should be borne in mind during preparation of the papers.

8. As the hearing is likely to be brief, the court may need to be taken through each of the proposed terms and directed individually to whether they should be made on an interim basis. Equally, the power of arrest will need justification on an interim injunction. Reference needs to be made to the individual acts which underlie the request for such an order.

Standard of proof for interim hearings and the balance of convenience

9. At the interim hearing, it may be worth reminding the court that, at this stage, it does not need to find the antisocial behaviour proved on the balance of probabilities. Indeed, such a finding would prejudice the final hearing if the same judge deals with it, because they could be accused of having formed a premature view of the evidence without properly considering it.

10. As a result, the court should be content to work on the basis that the interim injunction may be granted if the court is satisfied to the same standard as required for other interim injunctions. There is a well-known case in which the court set out a helpful test roughly equating to the phrase "*satisfied that it is just to grant an interim injunction*"[105].

11. Those principles in *American Cyanamid* are well known to every judge:

- the applicant must establish a serious issue to be tried;
- damages are not an adequate remedy;

[105] *American Cyanamid V Ethicon* [1975] AC 396, UKHL 1

- the balance of convenience lies in favour of granting the injunction, in that the order will do more good than harm;

- an undertaking in damages can be given (although this is not relevant to most ASB cases and care should be taken to strike through the sentence in the N16 form).

12. Although these criteria are not strictly applicable, because the test is expressed in the Act, if those first three requirements can be satisfied it is likely that a judge will be satisfied that it is just to grant an injunction.

13. There are a few points which are worth bearing in mind:

    - if there is no arguable defence there is no need to consider where the balance of convenience lies;

    - if there are no issues of fact then the court should not apply the principles but resolve the dispute before deciding whether to grant the application. In practice this will mean that if the ASB is admitted, the court might be urged to grant an injunction on a summary basis without hearing evidence;

    - if granting an injunction will effectively dispose of the claim, because by the time it comes on the trial there will be nothing worth fighting about, the court has to look beyond the balance of convenience and form a view as to who will win at trial.

14. It's very rare that a judge will mention the case, but defendants may rely on the above to say that an interim injunction would cause such prejudice to their client that an interim order should not be imposed. Most of the time that is unlikely to succeed, because injunctions usually simply prevent defendants from carrying out acts which are unlawful in any event.

15. There is an important exception: in cases where an exclusion is sought, particularly from a home, the test is important at an interim stage as already discussed:

- Extreme caution should be exercised by the applicant and the court before any application is pursued on an interim basis to exclude a defendant from their home.

- Equally, if the order has the effect of e.g., preventing a defendant from working or seeing their family, thought needs to be given to limiting the terms to the minimum necessary to protect the rights of others.

Terms of the order

16. If the judge is persuaded to grant an interim injunction, the exact terms of the order must be recorded in writing and signed by the judge before they are finalised, sealed and copied by the court. The order must set out clearly what the respondent must do or not do.[106]

17. A return date needs to be fixed after consideration of the nature of the injunction and whether an exclusion/a power of arrest has been imposed, whether it is likely to be strongly contested, the number of defendants, the size of the bundle etc.

18. Some judges will allocate a minimum of 30 minutes for any return date and it is not uncommon for the hearing to be listed for an hour if there is any complexity. The length of the return date will often dictate how soon after the interim hearing it will come back to court.

[106] CPR PD 25A para 5.5

Duration of the interim order

19. Many judges will make the interim order last for a fixed period, measured in years as envisaged by the application for the final order, adding the words "or until further order". Although this does not accord with the wording of the Act, it is simpler in practice, because if that interim order is approved unamended at a final hearing, it is unnecessary to draw up a fresh injunction order.

20. This does give rise to a technical but perhaps irritating prevalence of final orders which remain on the N16 form for an interim injunction order, with its superfluous wording about further hearings and so on.

Undertakings for damages

21. The CPR require any injunction order, unless the court orders otherwise, to contain an undertaking by the applicant to pay damages which a respondent sustains which the court considers the applicant should pay.[107] It is important to delete this undertaking from the draft order, as it is not appropriate for antisocial behaviour claims.[108]

Directions

22. At the hearing the court will need to make directions for the conduct of the return date.

---

[107] CPR PD 25A.5.1 (1) and 5.1A

[108] *Kirklees Metropolitan Borough Council v Wickes Building Supplies Ltd* [1993] AC 227, *Securities and Investments Board v Lloyd Wright* [1993] 4 All ER 210

Witness statement of defendant and further witness statements

23. The directions may deal with service of evidence in reply from the defendant and witnesses, of further evidence by the claimant's existing and other witnesses, and of other documentary evidence.

24. It is helpful to fix a date for service of the defendant's evidence as early as possible so that the applicant knows what is disputed and why. Evidence in reply can then be obtained if necessary.

Disclosure of documents

25. The court may make an order for the mutual disclosure by the parties of documents relevant to the application. The CPR address the way in which that should be done.[109]

26. Rather than going to the expense of preparing a formal disclosure list, the parties can ask the court to make an order that each disclose the documents on which they rely and which may be prejudicial to them/helpful to the other side.

Scott Schedule

27. If a Scott Schedule has not already been prepared, where there are more than a few allegations, the claimant should offer to create one. See Chapter Three for further details.

Medical evidence

28. If the defendant wishes to adduce any medical evidence, it is essential to ask for an order for disclosure of their relevant medical records. The claimant will need records going back at least to any period where any disability is alleged to have arisen. In some cases

[109] CPR 31

it may be possible to limit medical evidence to a report from a GP, but the records should still be sought and disclosed.

29. The court may insist on the appointment of a Single Joint Expert. If psychological or psychiatric evidence is requested, care should be taken before agreeing the appointment of any expert who works only for defendants. Consideration should be given to instructing an expert on behalf of the claimant, to scrutinise the report by the SJE and suggest possible questions for them.

30. In some cases, if the report by the SJE or the defendant's expert is wrong or misleading, it may be necessary to instruct an expert on behalf of the claimant. Care needs to be taken to make sure that experts are fully aware of the factual allegations.

Preparing a draft of the order

31. Directions will need to be reduced into a draft order, to be approved and signed by the judge either as part of the interim injunction order on the form N16 or on a separate General Form of Order. If the court prepares the order, the wording should be checked against the judge's draft.

32. Court staff are frequently so overworked that they may struggle to produce the order on the same day and sometimes within any reasonable period if they are not provided with a draft and reminded of the urgency. The resulting delays can mean an order is not produced for days or weeks.

33. Consequently, it is best to take a laptop to court to amend the draft order and email it to the court for printing or bring a portable printer to court. The judge can then approve the emailed or printed copy, sign it and have it sealed on the same day. Every court building now has Professional Court Users' Wi-Fi, which can be used by any legal professional.

34. When the judge makes the order, they will either (preferably) call listing during the hearing and ask a date or will mark the court file with a request that the listing officer should find the first date on which there is sufficient time available.

Service of the interim injunction order

35. Care must be taken when the order is obtained that service is properly made and evidence of that fact is gathered.

36. After the hearing, when the interim order is received from the court, it should be personally served unless the court orders otherwise under rule 6. The court can either approve service by an alternative method under CPR 6.27 and 6.15 or dispense with service of the paper order under CPR 6.28 as it is satisfied that the defendant is aware of the terms of the order.

37. The court can also proceed when no application has been made in accordance with CPR 81.6, but it will still have to issue a summons.

38. Subsequently, before allowing an arrest to take place or applying to commit for contempt, it is essential to check again that the order, in the form it is sought to enforce, was properly served on the defendant, or an alternative means of bringing it to his attention was authorised.

39. Further there must be good evidence of that service, in the form of a Certificate of Service complying with CPR 6.29, preferably accompanied by a witness statement setting out what happened when the defendant was served, giving evidence as to facts showing that the defendant understood the terms of the order.

40. The provisions of CPR 81 are of critical importance when dealing with defendants who evade service when a committal application is envisaged. Several problems are commonly encountered at enforcement stage:

- defendants refuse to accept that they have been served because they have not taken the papers from the process server but have let them drop to the ground at their feet;

- they claim that it was not them who accepted the papers-but a relative or friend;

- they evade the process server and, if they are not a professional who knows how to serve, the documents are nearly left in a post-box or similar;

- defendants claim that they are unable to read or otherwise had some reason why they could not understand the proceedings, or that the papers were destroyed by someone or something else.

41. The court has the power either to dispense with service or to make an order for service by an alternative method or at an alternative place, as discussed above.[110]

42. This is an important provision. It allows for retrospective dispensation with service, as well as an anticipatory order providing that the claimant can serve by an alternative means.

43. Service by an alternative means could include telling the defendant orally, service by text, or private message on Facebook or other social media, by serving or even telling a partner or relative. Obviously the more nebulous the means of service, the less inclined a judge will be to commit a defendant who denies knowing of an injunction.

44. However, all is not necessarily lost even if a defendant was not personally served and service was not dispensed with. The court may still enforce an order if it can be proved that the defendant

[110] CPR 6.15, 27 and 28

was aware of the terms and knew that their behaviour was a breach of the order.

45. This is pertinent if a defendant was in court when the order was made and there is a record of the judge informing them of its terms and confirming that they understood the requirements of the order and the penalty for breach.

Undertakings in lieu of an injunction

46. Often defendants and occasionally the court may suggest that it is appropriate that the court takes an undertaking from the defendant rather than imposing an injunction.

47. Most of the time an application will include a request that a power of arrest be attached to at least one provision of the injunction. A power of arrest cannot be attached to an undertaking. Additionally, an undertaking can be withdrawn by a defendant, necessitating the revival of the injunction application.

48. Therefore it is ill-advised to accept an undertaking unless the evidence is so weak that the claim for an injunction with power of arrest is likely to fail or the claimant is not really concerned about timely enforcement.

49. In cases where no power of arrest has been sought in the application, it may be appropriate to accept an undertaking. However, a claimant cannot subsequently ask the court to attach a power of arrest to the undertaking or to issue a warrant of arrest for any breach.

50. Further, Ground 7A cannot be used in possession proceedings. Again, it follows that there will be few circumstances in which it is appropriate to accept an undertaking.

51. A defendant must be personally present in court to give an undertaking and should not be allowed to provide one completed and signed elsewhere, as it will not be enforceable.

52. Additionally, once they have signed the General Form of Undertaking, a copy of it must be served on them.

CHAPTER NINE
APPLICATIONS WITHOUT NOTICE

KEY POINTS

1. Pre-conditions for without notice applications
2. Hearings before the claim is issued
3. Procedure
4. Paying the fee
5. "Ex-parte on notice" applications
6. Duty of full disclosure
7. Content of a draft without notice order
8. The without-notice hearing
9. The decision of the court
10. Obtaining the order after the hearing
11. Service of the order
12. Under 18's and consultation requirements

Pre-conditions for without notice applications

1. Usually an injunction is sought after a series of incidents and both parties know that an application is on the cards. The defendant will normally have been warned that if they do not modify their behaviour, action will be taken. An ABC or other informal or non-legal remedies may have been attempted.

2. Occasionally a defendant will do something which is so serious that there is no opportunity to attempt to avoid injunctive proceedings, or their behaviour may worsen suddenly. Sometimes there is reason to believe that, when served with the application papers, a perpetrator may act against witnesses.

3. Without notice applications are particularly useful if there is a risk that the defendant would, if notified of the application, act in a certain way and defeat the purpose of it before injunctive relief can be claimed. An obvious example is where there is a risk of witness intimidation, either by retaliatory threats or violence, or by attempts to dissuade someone from giving evidence. The same applies to applications without notice in which there is sufficient time to issue an application for an injunction.

4. In these cases, there is an obvious urgency and/or the need to prevent the defendant from finding out about the application before protection is provided to the victims.

5. Section 6 of the Act specifically allows for the making of an application without notice and gives the court three (and only three) alternatives when dealing with that application: it must (1) **adjourn** the proceedings,(a) **with or** (b) **without** an interim order *or* (3) it **must** dismiss the whole application.[111]

[111] Section 6 (2) (a)-(c)

6. If it adjourns the proceedings without an interim order, it is likely to be because there was insufficient evidence of the need for an ex-parte injunction. That could be as a result of failures in evidence gathering or presentation, because there is no demonstrable need for an order before service, or simply because of a failure in advocacy at the hearing.

7. It follows that it is important to make applications without notice only when the facts deserve them. The circumstances in which that is the case are obvious to an experienced practitioner, so it is quite understandable that the less experienced should discuss any intended application with others and come to a reasoned decision before acting.

8. Applications can be made after business hours and at weekends. The court will require an undertaking to be offered to issue the claim immediately after the hearing, or as soon as the court opens for normal business hours. The email or letter accompanying the application should explain briefly the circumstances and the urgency of the situation.

9. If the only reason that it can be said to be urgent is that insufficient effort has been made to issue a claim, the court is likely to think carefully before granting any relief without notice. Any failure or mistake by a claimant should be admitted in the original application, as the applicant has a duty of full disclosure to the court.

Application and hearing before a claim is issued

10. If the application is made before the claim has even been issued, the rules say that the court can grant relief if it is urgent *or* it is

otherwise desirable to do so in the interests of justice,[112] which must be read in conjunction with section 4 of the Act.

Procedure

11. It is necessary to inform the court at the earliest possible moment of the impending application. Subsequently, if there has been time to draft any papers, they can be filed as they are prepared, either electronically or in a bundle as the court requires. If providing paper copies, three copies of the application, evidence in support and draft order will need to be printed if possible, with additional copies for extra defendants.

12. As with on-notice applications, a draft of the order needs to be provided electronically and the order as made by the judge should be typed by the applicant and emailed to the court, or printed at court.

CPR 23 and the Practice Direction

13. CPR 23.4 also allows for applications to be made without notice in all proceedings. The Practice Direction[113] says that applications can be made without notice only where there is "*exceptional urgency*", where the overriding objective is "*best furthered by doing so*", by consent or by permission of the court or where some other rule etc provides for it. Those are quite useful factors to have in mind when considering an application without notice, as the court will relate to the phrases.

14. The facts relied on as to why the application has been made without notice should be made plain at the earliest stage possible, both in the N16A and in the witness evidence.

---

[112] CPR 25.2 (2) (b)

[113] CPR PD 23A.3

15. Although the court is rarely referred to authorities at and after without-notice hearings, it is worth knowing the basis on which the court will act in other areas of the law. The general principle is that they will only be granted in cases of "exceptional urgency", especially if they are made out of hours.[114] The reasons for asking for an order without notice should be set out as soon as possible in the witness statement.

16. Although a claimant's own delay in making an application is not likely to be looked upon favourably, where the beneficiaries of an injunction will not be a claimant itself but, for instance nearby residents or employees, the court may be prepared to take a more forgiving view of what might otherwise be a culpable failure to act swiftly. Any delays must be admitted and reasons given, even if it is simply by way of an apology for inexcusable inaction.

17. In some exceptional cases it might be wise to state in the application or accompanying letter that, if the court is not satisfied that an order should be made without notice in the terms sought, either:

- a modified or limited order is requested, or
- the court should list the without notice application as "ex-parte on notice" the following day (see below) or
- the court is asked to grant part of the application and adjourn the remainder for a short time (between hours and a day or two) to allow the defendant to be served and to attend court.

18. In all cases, the evidence should be drafted recognising that the application will be brought back for a return date hearing within a short period-often between a few days and a couple of weeks,

[114] *Franses v Al Assad and Ors* [2007] EWHC 2442 (Ch), para 67

after the defendant has been served with the interim without notice order. It may be worth reminding the court in the evidence that the interim, a without notice order is only sought for a matter of days, to protect the witnesses pending a more considered hearing. Care must also be taken to draft the order so that it provides sufficient protection to witnesses in the interim.

19. The aim is to provide a level of protection for witnesses which is meaningful. In a case where there have been significant threats which might be carried out, it may be necessary to ask for protection in the form of a power of arrest and/or exclusion from a particular area. Care is needed in the collection and presentation of the evidence relied on to support any requests for any apparently draconian relief, given the restrictions which the Court of Appeal have placed on claimants seeking exclusion orders and powers of arrest, particularly without notice.

Paying the fee

20. It is necessary to pay the fee at the time of issue and courts are unlikely to accept undertakings from unknown litigants to pay fees in due course. Organisations which have an account with the court will be able to avoid issues caused by an inability to provide payment.

"Ex-parte on notice" applications

21. An application may also be made "ex-parte on notice", in circumstances where there may be some doubt as to whether an application entirely without notice is appropriate. There is some support for such applications in the CPR themselves, in that CPR PD 25 a Para 4.3 (3) provides that "*except in cases where secrecy is essential, the applicant should take steps to notify the respondent informally of the application*".

22. This course of action can have disadvantages. If short notice is given to a respondent, particularly if it is plainly insufficient to

allow them to prepare properly, the court cannot expect them to have done so and is more likely to adjourn issues on which the respondent says they are in need of extra time. The applicant still has to give full and frank disclosure in respect of all the issues on which the respondent has not had time to prepare fully.[115]

23. The procedure is particularly useful if an application is being made to exclude a defendant from their home at very short notice. If they can be informed of the forthcoming application, and even brought to court if necessary, problems such as those which arose in *Moat* can be avoided.

Duty of full disclosure

24. Every applicant for relief who does not give notice to the respondent is under a "compelling duty" to make full and frank disclosure to the court.[116] It is essential to bear that duty in mind in the preparation of the evidence to be relied on.

25. This obligation applies equally to material which detracts from the strength of the claim (such as knowledge that a witness for the claimant has criminal convictions for dishonesty) and which may be actively beneficial to a respondent's potential case (e.g. a medical report received by the claimant which explains the behaviour and provides a disability discrimination defence).

26. Those points should be mentioned and dealt with in the witness evidence and the applicant needs to anticipate what Judge would think is material. As the application progresses, make sure that anything which you feel it is your duty to disclose to the court is

---

115 *CEF Holdings Ltd and Another v Mundey & Others* [2012] EWHC 1524, para 174-183

116 *Memory Corporation PLC v Sidhu (No 2)* [2000] EWCA Civ 9, [2000] 1 WLR 1443 at 1459 H to 1460 B

noted and recorded. If there is any doubt, disclose it to avoid later criticism.

27. The effect of non-disclosure can be dramatic-if your opponent accuses you of hiding material from the court, they may ask the judge to set the order side simply because of the failure to disclose, rather than on the merits. Although nondisclosure used to result in automatic discharge of an injunction granted without notice, that is no longer the case in general and there is no rule specific to antisocial behaviour cases.

28. Nowadays the court needs to ask itself whether the non-disclosure would have resulted in the order not being made originally. If an order would have been made in any event even if the disclosure had been made, the court has a choice whether to continue the order, or make it on different terms. If nondisclosure is deliberate, that will incline the court toward discharging the injunction. There may be other facts which are relevant to the question whether it should be discharged, e.g. how quick the applicant was to admit the nondisclosure and whether it has been put right.

29. Further, antisocial behaviour cases are different to the normal legal claim, in that the beneficiary of an order is rarely the claimant itself, so discharge of an order would have an effect on those other than the party responsible.

30. At the same time as making full disclosure, the person attending the hearing needs to be ready to make a full note of both the submissions and the judgement. In theory this should be served on the respondent, although in practice applicants rarely do so.

Content of a draft without notice order

31. If an order is sought without notice, the rules say that the draft must contain an undertaking by the applicant to serve the respondent with the documents as soon practicable, a space to

insert the return date for the hearing and an undertaking to file and, if made before filing an application notice, to pay the appropriate fee.[117]

The without-notice hearing

32. Some applicants attend the hearing themselves, appearing by their officers if the claim is housing related. Employees appearing in court should remind themselves of the duty of full disclosure and this is particularly so on hearings without notice.

33. The court will often have to fit an urgent hearing into an already busy list. Brevity in presenting the application is essential. This must be balanced against the possibility that an opponent might later take advantage of any apparent breach of that duty of full disclosure.

34. It is essential to draw to the attention of the judge any reasons why they may need to exercise caution before imposing particular terms of the injunction on a without notice basis. This is especially important when asking for a power of arrest and even more so when asking for an exclusion. At first hearing without notice applicants should be cautious before pursuing either.

35. Familiarity with *Moat* is essential, and the court should be reminded of the restrictions imposed by the Court of Appeal on the grant of such orders. It is one thing to obtain either term in an order without notice, but another to justify at a return date why the court was not reminded of those restrictions. If there is any concern about the potential for subsequent criticism, it is best dealt with by refraining from demanding onerous terms but in any event asking for an early return date.

[117] CPR PD 25A.5.1, paras (2)-(4)

36. Additionally, if a power of arrest or exclusion is sought ex parte, it is possible to avoid any potential for significant injustice by ensuring that the Return Date is brought forward to a time only a day or two after the without notice hearing.

37. Poor preparation or an inability to explain the basis on which the order is sought can lead to the court adjourning the application with no order, or even dismissing it.

38. If the application is adjourned and, before the return date, the defendant causes further nuisance, intimidates or threatens witnesses etc, this should be brought to the attention of the court. Admissible evidence needs to be obtained, filed and served, no matter how close to the hearing.

39. The without-notice hearing may have the appearance of being less formal because the defendant is not present, but an advocate should not be lulled into a false sense of security as the hearing will be recorded and may subsequently be transcribed.

40. If the hearing has been squeezed into a busy list, the judge may not even have had an opportunity to read the papers. The court should be taken briefly through the order sought, the reasons for the application and the evidence behind it.

41. No oral evidence is heard at interim hearings. Witness statements can be accepted as evidence of the facts in them and the judge makes the decision based on those statements unless they are inherently incredible. The witnesses do not need to attend court. However, in some cases it can be helpful if they do so, as they may wish to see the inside of the court before giving evidence or they may be able to help with issues arising or questions asked by the judge.

42. If there are any issues which are unusual or are likely to be contentious, they should be brought to the attention of the judge

and a note made of the observations of the court with regard to those issues.

43. At without-notice hearings the applicant may decide not to pursue certain prohibitions or other aspects of the claim. This should be clearly stated, preferably in writing before the hearing. If pursuing a power of arrest or exclusion, written submissions are advisable so that the defendant is able to understand the reasons for the making of an apparently Draconian order.

44. At a without notice hearing, the order cannot require a defendant to participate in any activity.[118]

The decision of the court and drawing up the order

45. The court will make a decision on whether to grant an interim order, adjourn the interim application or to dismiss it.

46. It is then the responsibility of the claimant to ensure that the order is drawn up to reflect the intention of the judge. Some judges will prefer to draft the order themselves and get the court to seal it, others will expect the claimant to take charge. It is desirable to be armed with a laptop and a copy of the draft order in Word.

Obtaining the order after the hearing

47. The sealed order will be provided with a Notice of Hearing, giving the date of time of the Return Date and a time estimate. The judge may have made additional directions to be complied with by both parties before the next hearing.

48. In theory, notes of the hearing should be subsequently provided to the other side. In practice this is nearly always overlooked.

---

[118] section 7 (3)

Service of the order

49. Once the sealed order is obtained from the court, it is necessary to serve it in the same way as an order obtained on notice (see earlier on service). Obviously, as a defendant will be unaware of the impending proceedings, care must be taken to explain the reasons behind the order and the terms on which it was made.

50. This can be done by way of a formal visit to a defendant, recorded by the claimant and confirmed by subsequent letter to them. A Certificate of Service and accompanying witness statement should also be obtained. Everything the defendant says or does should be recorded as part of a witness statement. It can be particularly useful to be able to prove e.g. that the defendant understood the order or that they attempted to evade service.

51. The return date will follow the course of an interim hearing on notice, although if it is listed before the same Judge the court will obviously be familiar with the facts. The background will only need repetition so far as the defendant needs to be informed of the circumstances of and reasons for the application. For this reason, if the application is complex, it may be wise to attempt to have the return date listed before the same District Judge.

Under 18's and consultation requirements

52. When an application is being made without notice against an under 18-year-old, there is no need to consult other bodies. Clearly such an obligation would slow things down and the defendant might inadvertently be alerted to the forthcoming proceedings.

53. However, after the without notice hearing, the consultation must take place before the first hearing on notice.[119]

[119] Section 4 (2)

CHAPTER TEN
THE FINAL HEARING

KEY POINTS

1. Potential issues in final hearings
2. Applications to stay pending criminal proceedings
3. Preparation for final hearing
4. Disclosure
5. Hearsay evidence at the trial
6. Evidence of breaches
7. Trial bundle preparation
8. Case summary, skeleton argument and chronology
9. Special measures for witnesses
10. Establishing the grounds for the final order
11. Costs
12. Appeals
13. Publicising the Order

1. A final hearing will be necessary if a respondent has not accepted that an injunction is merited at all, or has contested certain of the terms sought and a compromise cannot be reached. In a final

hearing, the court will be considering whether to continue the interim injunction already granted, to extend or to discharge it.

Potential issues in final hearings

2. Disputes of both fact and law can be raised by a defendant in their witness statement in reply to the application. The preparation additional to that required for an interim hearing will obviously depend on the nature of the issues remaining in contention.

3. The defendant may raise disputes of fact, alleging that witnesses are lying or mistaken.[120] A defendant may claim mistaken identity, alibi, or just accuse the claimant's witnesses of lying. Often it will be necessary to obtain evidence in reply to the defendant's assertions.

4. Therefore, on receipt of a defendant's witness statements, the claimant's witnesses should be asked about what they contain. They will frequently provide useful additional details which show that a defendant must be lying or mistaken in their defence.

Applications to stay a claim pending criminal proceedings

5. Occasionally defendants will object to the grant of an injunction or other civil claim against their client on the basis that the defendant is facing criminal proceedings and advancing civil claims at the same time will prejudice them.

6. There is no general right to stay proceedings, based on any privilege against self-incrimination or any other reason.[121] A defendant has to identify and prove on the balance of

---

[120] *see for example Festival Housing Ltd v Baker* [2017] EW Misc 4 (CC)

[121] *Jefferson Ltd v Betcha* [1979] 2 All ER 1108

probabilities the "*respects in which the continuance of civil proceedings may prejudice the criminal trial*".[122]

7. Even when there is a real risk of prejudice to a defendant if the civil proceedings are heard first, it is still no guarantee that the injunction proceedings will be stopped.[123]

8. The claimant can oppose such applications by offering procedural safeguards against prejudice, e.g. by excluding police officers from the court during evidence and submissions, by conceding a ban on publicity pending the criminal trial, or by making sure witnesses do not 'cross-contaminate' each other.

Preparation for the hearing

9. The trial differs from interim hearings in one fundamental aspect: evidence is not normally received by way of written statement without consent or reliance on the 1995 Act. If facts remain in dispute, then subject to the hearsay rules, oral evidence will be heard by the court.

10. This means that preparation for a final hearing is likely to be more complex and the hearing will probably last longer. Directions for trial will have been given at the on-notice hearing and usually half a day or a day set is aside for the final hearing.

Disclosure

11. In standard disclosure the test is whether the documents are relied on by a party, or they adversely affect the party's own case or that of another party, or even support another party's case.

[122] CPR PD 23 A.11 A, which also requires a defendant (or a prosecutor or other applicant) to make a formal application to the court for a stay

[123] *Re DPR Futures* [1989] 1 WLR 778

Additionally, a party must disclose anything which is required to be disclosed by a relevant practice direction.

12. It is easy to overlook the scope of those documents which are required. They include inconsistent statements by witnesses, any previous convictions relevant to the credibility of a witness, evidence of steps taken in the decision to make an application for an injunction etc.

13. Sometimes documents come to light during the disclosure process which are potentially embarrassing or detrimental to the claim. They must still be disclosed. It is necessary to question whether they do in fact damage the application.

14. If a decision is taken that changes the merits, an applicant should not hesitate to change tack. Alternatively, if there is a good explanation why the document is not damaging, it should be given by way of a further witness statement. For example if it comes to light that a witness has previous convictions which appear to be relevant, they should be asked about them.

Hearsay evidence at the trial

15. Ideally, by the time of the trial, the witnesses will be willing to attend court and give evidence, even if they were reluctant to do so beforehand.

16. If witnesses remain unwilling to give evidence and the defendant serves a witness statement contesting the hearsay evidence, effort will need to be made to prove the facts in that hearsay evidence.

17. A defendant is likely to rely on the words of Brooke LJ in *Harris v Moat Housing* at para 135:

> "… *the willingness of a civil court to admit hearsay evidence carries with it inherent dangers… Rumours abound in a small housing estate, and it is much more difficult for a judge to assess*

the truth of what he is being told of the original maker of the statement does not attend court to be cross-examined on his/her evidence."

18. If possible, corroboration of the evidence should be obtained, so that the court gives the evidence due weight. Examples might include getting multiple unnamed witnesses to provide anonymous witness statements relating to the same events, obtaining copies of police reports, witness statements, photographs of exhibits etc, medical records, CCTV photographs and video and criminal convictions.

19. But just because a witness refuses to come to court, the applicant should not give up trying to rely on their evidence. A Civil Evidence notice should be served, giving the reason why they are unwilling to attend (often because they are terrified of the defendant, but see generally Chapter 4 on the preparation of evidence) and the evidence should be included in the trial bundle.

Evidence of breaches

20. In the interim, the defendant may well have breached the injunction on one or more occasion. Arrests and subsequent committal proceedings frequently predate the final hearing. Thus, by the time the trial is listed, the result can be a foregone conclusion.

21. However, even if no committal proceedings have taken place, evidence of breaches is still highly pertinent to the question whether a final injunction should be granted, and if so on what terms.

Trial bundle preparation

22. Bundles for the hearing need to be prepared in the same way as for interim hearings, though there is likely to be significantly

more material and care should be taken to separate it into manageably sized dividers.

23. If the hearing is remote, the PDF bundle must follow the Practice Direction and the various requirements found in other sources on how to prepare such bundles. It is an art form, and they are difficult to get right. They must at the very least be paginated otherwise than by hand, and indexed, with bookmarks.

Case summary, skeleton argument and chronology

24. Such documents are helpful to the court and the advocates. It may be possible to agree principles of law with an opponent, to avoid bombarding the court with authorities.

Special measures to protect witnesses

25. Well before the hearing at which a frightened or vulnerable witness is expected to attend, consideration should be given whether to ask the court for measures to be taken to protect them.

26. Section 16 of the Act allows the court to make a "special measures direction", which might allow for the giving of evidence from behind a screen, by video link or in private.

27. The application does not have to be made formally-the applicant can write to the court requesting such measures, copying in the defendant or their representatives.

28. Prior to the hearing it is wise to remind the court that special measures have been requested and to attend very early to ensure that the court staff have time to prepare court room or check the video link as appropriate.

29. Such measures are surprisingly helpful – defendants who intimidate witnesses outside court by swearing at or abusing them can have a significant effect on their confidence in court.

30. A screen may not be needed to protect the witness for the entire time they are in court-it is often enough simply to use it when the witnesses giving evidence. Video links are notoriously unreliable and should be a last resort.

31. If the defendant turns up in court with followers or family who misbehave, the court may entertain an informal application to exclude them from the hearing.

32. The final hearing of an injunction application should resemble any other civil trial, subject to the existence of witness protection measures.

33. It may be necessary to 'open' the application so that the judge is aware of the grounds on which is made and the facts which give rise to the need for each term of the proposed order. Witnesses will then be called and the claimant will 'close' its case. The defendant then decides whether they will give evidence. Speeches and judgement follow.

Establishing the grounds for the final order

34. The court will make findings in its judgement, and they should be recorded in the preamble to the final injunction order.

Compliance with the Protocol

35. When the Protocol comes into force, part of its findings will relate to compliance. Normally, one would hope that this can amount to a brief statement that the PAP was complied with, or that any breaches were not significant. Alternatively, that they may have been significant, but it would be inappropriate to restrict the terms of the order, or to refuse to make it. Equally, the court will only impose sanctions such as costs at the judgment stage if the defendant has alleged and proved that the failure to comply was unreasonable.

36. It is to be hoped that arguments as to whether there has been compliance will not give rise to overlong hearings, or to disproportionate argument when there is a clear need for an injunction. However, experience from other protocols would suggest that these issues are likely to become another unwelcome form of satellite litigation.

Findings of fact

37. Turning to the substantive application, any findings on the allegations of ASB should be recorded by way of a Schedule.

38. The court will be converting the interim injunction made under section 7 of the Act to a final order made under section 1.

39. The difference between the tests bears repetition. The interim order was made simply because the court thought it just to do so. The final order will be made upon:

    - proof of allegations on the balance of probabilities and

    - the court considering it just and convenient to make the injunction (which will now include an assessment of compliance with the Pre-Action Protocol);

    - to prevent the respondent from engaging in ASB (i.e. specific types of behaviour).

40. It is to those paragraphs that any defendant will address their efforts to prevent the making of an order or to influence the terms on which it is made.

Evidential issues

41. A defendant may challenge the admission of evidence in various ways and it is necessary to be familiar with the principles of the law of evidence. A good example is identification evidence.

42. A defendant may say that little weight should be placed on the identification by a witness of a defendant based on an allegedly 'fleeting glimpse'. Sometimes this may genuinely have been a momentary and possibly unsatisfactory sighting of an individual presumed to be a defendant, but sometimes there is no reason to doubt that identification.[124]

43. The judgment will need to set out why the court is satisfied that the applicant has proved on the balance of probabilities the allegations in question.

Standard of proof

44. Proof on the balance of probabilities is not a difficult test to satisfy, particularly if not all the evidence is hearsay.

Just and convenient

45. This has been examined in Chapter Two. The court will need to refer to the test in the judgment. When the Protocol comes into force, the court will consider any non-compliance as part of the test whether it is just and convenient to make the order.

46. That assessment, it is suggested, should involve a weighing up of the effects of any breach. By the time of the final hearing, it is to be hoped that any non-compliance by either party will have been remedied and it will not be an issue.

47. It would be unfortunate if the effect of the introduction of the Protocol resulted in an emasculation of the 2014 Act. However, drawing from experience of the equality legislation, the PAP is likely to lengthen and complicate proceedings, which of itself prejudices victims.

---

[124] See for instance how the judge dealt with such a submission in *Knightstone Housing v Pugh* [2016] EW Misc B31 at para 12-17

Prevention of ASB

48. Clearly if there are reasons why an injunction is not necessary to achieve the protection of others from ASB, the court will be unable to make the final order.

49. There may be obvious reasons why it might not be appropriate to make a final order, such as (1) the defendant being a serving prisoner who will not be released in the foreseeable future, (2) the source of the nuisance may have been removed, e.g. a defendant tenant may have evicted their misbehaving visitor or family member, or (3) the defendant may have beaten an alcohol or drug addiction or may have otherwise reformed.

50. Such events may well have occurred since the application was made, so care should be taken to protect the applicant's position on costs (see below).

51. Additionally, the terms of the order might subject to challenge, both in ambit and nature. The court will need to address any matters raised by the defendant, and consider how wide to make the injunction, on what terms and for how long those matters are in dispute.

Costs

52. if an applicant succeeds on an application, although many defendants will have limited resources, it's important to ask for costs orders, particularly because, unless the defendant is legally aided, they can be set off against any subsequent costs order which might be made against the claimant.

53. The applicant can ask for summary assessment of the costs if they have served a Statement of Costs. If not, it is still possible to ask for costs, to be assessed if not agreed, although in the absence of service of a Statement of Costs the court might not agree to the making of any order.

54. If a defendant succeeds in an argument that the order should not be made, or that it should be made on different terms, it will rarely be appropriate to make an order for costs against the applicant.

55. Authorities charged with the protection of the public should not normally be made to pay the costs of an unsuccessful application which strives to achieve that aim. An exception might be aware the application has been unreasonable, or in some way clearly inappropriate.

Appeals

56. When the Act first came into force there were a few appeals against orders made. Appeals against the imposition of orders are rare, probably because applicants are careful to issue claims only where action is needed and the parties ensure that first instance that the terms imposed are appropriate.

57. In any event, if it subsequently transpires that variation of the injunction would be in the interests of justice, the parties frequently agree changes, or allow the judge to determine an informal application for variation.

58. County Court decisions are appealed to the High Court and an appeal is made adhering to the provisions of CPR 52.

59. The Act contains provision125 for the making of an appeal against a decision of the Youth Court. Either side may appeal to the Crown Court, which then has jurisdiction to make

section 15

directions[126] and any "whatever incidental or consequential orders appear to it to be just".

60. In the appeal any order made other than a direction that the application is to be re-heard by the Youth Court will be treated for the purposes of the Act as an order of the Youth Court.

Publicising the order

61. The government considered it useful for applicants to be able to inform the public of the making of antisocial behaviour injunctions. As a result, reporting restrictions in relation to under 18-year-olds[127] are specifically disapplied by the Act,[128] The court retains a discretion under section 39 of the CYPA 1933 to restrict the publication of the personal details of the respondent.

62. In practice, it is advisable to resist any attempt to keep such details private unless there is a fear it will lead to significant harm to a young person.

---

126 section 15 (2)

127 imposed by section 49 of the Children and Young Persons Act 1933

128 Section 17

CHAPTER ELEVEN

BREACHES – ARREST WITHOUT WARRANT AND CONTEMPT APPLICATIONS

KEY POINTS

1. Introduction
2. Preparation for the arrest
3. Forcible entry into premises
4. Arrest
5. Police station procedure
6. Defendants taken immediately to court
7. Presenting a defendant at court
8. Contempt applications under CPR 81
9. Applications on the court's own initiative
10. Service of contempt applications
11. Directions for hearing of contempt proceedings
12. Remedying breaches of CPR 81

Introduction

1. Breach of an injunction is a contempt of court. The Act does not provide for the penalty. Instead, disobedience with the court order is dealt with in the same way as a failure to obey other injunctions.

2. If a power of arrest was attached to the injunction it allows a constable to arrest the respondent without a warrant if they have "*reasonable cause to suspect that the respondent is in breach of (a) provision*" of the injunction.[129]

3. Alternatively, if the term of the injunction does not carry a power of arrest, an application to commit must be made, following the procedural requirements of CPR 81. The rules were substantially changed with effect from 1 October 2020. And the revocation of Practice Direction 81.

4. Whichever process is followed, before the court can punish a defendant for a contempt of court, it must find the breach proved and that any application to purge the contempt has failed. The new CPR 81, which came into force on 1 October 2020 provides the framework within which applicants must work in committal proceedings.

5. There are three ways in which a contempt application can be started: on an arrest with or without a warrant, and within a formal application for committal for contempt.

6. We will consider the position on arrest without a warrant (under a power of arrest) first, then deal with formal applications under CPR 81.4. Chapter Twelve deals with contempt following an application for a warrant of arrest.

---

[129] Section 9 (1)

Preparation for the arrest

7. Once the applicant hears of a breach, they need to check the facts and, only if there is good evidence of breach, contact the police. The victim(s) may already have notified the police of the breach.

8. Either way, it is important to ensure that the police are aware of all potential breaches of which there is evidence, rather than simply the most recent or most serious.

9. It is important to communicate by email a full list and details of the allegations, so that the police can arrest for every breach rather than just the one in respect of which they may have been called by the victim.

10. Equally, officers should be told very clearly which parts of the injunction do not carry a power of arrest, so that they do not make the mistake of making an unlawful arrest.

Forcible entry into premises

11. There is no explicit statutory power of entry associated with a power of arrest or the grant of a warrant of arrest. The County Court is a creature of statute, so a power of entry would not normally arise just because a judge has issued a warrant of arrest.

12. When making an order in pursuit of numerous other statutes and statutory instruments the courts have a statutory power[130] to order entry onto premises.

13. The police will not usually use force to enter a property to arrest for breach of an injunction, because breach of a civil injunction does not appear in the list, in section 17 of the Police and

[130] see the Protection of Freedoms Act 2012 documents: Powers of entry

Criminal Evidence Act 1984, of offences for which the police may forcibly enter.

14. If the defendant is wanted on other criminal charges, the defendant can be arrested at the same time as the warrant is executed or he is arrested for those offences, which may well include allegations justifying forced entry.

15. If a defendant refuses to allow the police to enter the property in order to arrest them, the claimant can try returning to court and ask the judge for an order specifically permitting the claimant and/or the police to use force to gain entry for the purposes of an arrest.

16. Alternatively if there is a term of the tenancy agreement permitting access for the purposes of enforcing the terms of the tenancy, an application might be pursued on that basis. A contractual right of forcible entry will not be inferred and needs to be clear.

17. The court may agree that it can justify forced entry to arrest under the inherent power of the court to authorise acts which are carried out in the course of enforcement of an order.

The arrest

18. When the police do arrest, if possible they should specify all the allegations or give the defendant a list of them. Alternatively, the police can simply arrest for "breach of injunction" generally. In this way the court is able to consider all the breaches without the necessity to issue a formal application to commit, which is obviously more time-consuming and expensive.

19. After arrest the police have a statutory duty to inform the applicant of the fact that they have arrested the defendant.[131] The police may need reminding of this obligation, which needs to be performed as soon as possible.

20. Immediately upon hearing of an arrest, it is the duty of the applicant to inform the court (NB not the police) – by email and/or telephone.

21. Sometimes the police tell the court themselves but may make the mistake of informing only the Magistrates' court.

22. Defendants aged under 18 have be taken to the Magistrates' court, where they can be dealt with by a Justice of the Peace and will be remanded to appear before the Youth Court which granted the injunction. Under 18-year-olds cannot be remanded in custody unless paragraph 6 of Schedule 1 (medical conditions) applies.

23. Once in custody, a defendant will either be taken to the police station or occasionally straight to court.

24. Before a defendant is transported to the cells it is essential that the court finds a judge and a courtroom in which the remand hearing can take place. Very occasionally a District Judge will hear a remand hearing at the police station. Following the pandemic, it has become more standard practice to conduct remand hearings from the police station by video link.

25. Some police forces will invite an ASB officer to attend the execution of a warrant or a drugs raid, which can provide much better evidence for the purposes of the County Court.

---

[131] Section 9 (2)

Police station procedure

26. The police are likely to administer a criminal caution to a defendant. For the purposes of the initial arrest, this will suffice. When at court, care must be taken to go further (see Chapter Fourteen on committal hearings).

27. Defendants are usually taken to the police station, but many Custody Officers are not familiar with the requirements of civil proceedings so will treat the allegation as a criminal charge. Although there is a right to silence, the similarities with the charging of an offence are otherwise limited. Despite this the police tend to describe the breach in the same language as that used in criminal proceedings, which can lead to confusion.

28. There is no formal obligation to interview a defendant, although it is extremely useful if the police do put the facts of the alleged breaches to the defendant in an interview under caution. That interview may elicit admissions which can later greatly reduce the cost and time involved in a committal.

29. Officers frequently fill in "MG 11" witness statements, which according to the CPR are not admissible in evidence in contempt proceedings. Despite this, many defendants do not take objection to this failure to comply with the CPR, particularly at the hearing following arrest.

30. Ideally the police should be asked to fill in a pro-forma affidavit instead, which can be sworn at a later date. In any event, all MG 11 witness statements must be exhibited to an affidavit if they are to be admissible as evidence in contempt proceedings. Officers should be asked to include the defendant's relevant criminal record/antecedents in the information they provide.

Defendants taken immediately to court

31. Sometimes rather than taking a defendant to a police station, the police will arrest and take a defendant to court immediately, for instance where the defendant has young children and is not possible to find anybody to look after them.

32. As long as the applicant has been informed of the intention to arrest, this is unlikely to be an issue. However, if the police arrest at short notice, as is likely after a serious incident, they may have limited time to notify others before they take the defendant into custody.

Presenting a defendant at court

33. Once the arrest has happened, the claimant has only 24 hours in which to present the defendant at court.[132] Whether the applicant was involved in arranging the arrest or it happened following an incident of which it had no prior notice, the defendant will often end up in custody overnight. The following morning, they must be brought to the court so that they can appear well within the 24-hour period.

34. This time limit can present a logistical problem. If the defendant is arrested before about midday, the applicant should ensure that they are either presented at court on the same day, or that arrangements are made with the court for the hearing to take place well before the expiry of the 24-hours at midday.

35. Court officers should be made aware of the urgency of the situation and explicitly given the time by which the defendant must be brought before the court, i.e. the hearing must begin less than 24 hours post-arrest. If time is likely to be tight,

[132] Section 9 (3), although Christmas Day, Good Friday and Sundays are disregarded. This does mean that a defendant must be produced on bank holidays and New Year's Day if arrested the day before.

consideration should be given to asking the court to deal with the hearing remotely.

36. Following the arrest and remand, the court has 28 days in which to deal with the contempt proceedings. Although it is technically possible to open the proceedings and adjourn part-heard to a date later than 28 days after arrest, it is bad practice to do so-breaches need to be dealt with swiftly if the injunction process is to have any teeth.

37. If the claimant is unable to arrest for breach of the injunction because there is no power of arrest attached to that term of the injunction, an application may be made for the issue of an arrest warrant. See Chapter Twelve.

Contempt applications under CPR 81

38. Alternatively, if there is no power of arrest and the applicant chooses not to ask for a warrant, an application for committal for contempt ("a contempt application") must be made, following the mandatory procedure in CPR 81.

The new provisions of CPR 81

39. CPR 81 contains 10 paragraphs and was intended to simplify contempt applications.

40. CPR 81.3 specifies that they are made under CPR 23 and should be heard by a Circuit Judge *unless there is a rule or practice direction allowing District Judges to hear them*[133]. They are permitted to hear committal applications in ASBI cases by CPR

[133] an amendment to the original version of CPR 81.3 (2) inserted by the civil procedure rules committee as a matter of urgency on 9 October 2020, following concern that the jurisdiction of district judges to hear committal proceedings had been mistakenly removed by the new rule

65.47 and Practice Direction 2B, which together mean they can hear committals:

41. Paragraph PD 2B 8.1 provides that:

> " ... *In the first instance, the following applications for orders and interim remedies (including injunctions whether interim or final) will be allocated to a District Judge – ...*
>
> *(c) injunctions that are to be made under any of the following provisions – ...*
>
> *(v) Part 1 of the Anti-Social Behaviour, Crime and Policing Act 2014.*

Para 8.3 says:

> *Any proceedings in which the court may make an order committing a person to prison or attach a power of arrest to an injunction or remand a person will be allocated to a Circuit Judge, unless the order, power of arrest or remand is made -*
>
> *(a) In proceedings which have been or may be allocated to a District Judge pursuant to paragraph 8.1 above...*"

42. Applications must comply with CPR 81.4 and be supported by affidavit or affirmation evidence. There is a new application form, the N600, which "*ought to be used unless there are compelling reasons justifying not doing so' since the 'form is standardised and has been framed, deliberately, to set out the information that is required to be provided under CPR 81.4(2) to ensure procedural fairness*" and "*contains important information to the respondent about his/her rights*".[134]

---

[134] See *MBR Acres Ltd v Maher (also known as John Thibeault), per Nicklin J*

It should:

- include statements of matters such as the nature of the nature of the breach, the date and terms of any order or undertaking breached, confirmation of personal service or dispensation that there was a notice on the order, and that the defendant understood its terms and the consequences of breach;

- set out a brief summary[135] of the facts, numerically in chronological order. It must inform the defendant that they have a right to be legally represented and to obtain legal aid, an interpreter and to reasonable time to prepare.

- tell the defendant that he is entitled but not obliged to give written and oral evidence in their defence but has the right to remain silent. It needs to inform the defendant that the court can proceed in their absence, and that if the breach is proved they can be fined, imprisoned, or have their assets confiscated or suffer other punishment[136];

- inform the defendant of their right to admit the contempt and apologise, which is likely to reduce the seriousness of any punishment, that the findings will be provided in writing as soon practicable after the hearing and the court will sit in public.

---

135 see the case (below) of Deutsche Bank AG v Sebastian Holdings Inc and anor [2020] EWHC 3536 (Comm) for what this means

136 note that a committal can proceed in the absence of a defendant but see *Newman v Modern Bookbinders* (2000) 2 All ER 814 CA for the procedural safeguards necessary.

43. As is usual with such PDF forms, they do not allow for automatic paragraph numbering and other sophisticated formatting unless converted to Word.

Applications on the court's own initiative

44. Also, note that even if a claimant does not make an application for committal, under CPR 81.6 if the court "*considers that a contempt of court... may have been committed, the court on its own initiative shall consider whether to proceed against the defendant in contempt proceedings.*" Thus in an appropriate case, you may suggest to the court that it proceeds of its own initiative.

45. If the court does so, CPR 81.6 provides that it can ask the parties to give such assistance as is proportionate unreasonable. It needs to issue a summons to the defendant, in the same terms as the new contempt application form.

Service of contempt applications

46. CPR 81.5 says that they must be served personally unless the court directs otherwise in accordance with Part 6, or they are served on the defendant's legal representative unless they object in writing within seven days of service, in which case the court will consider what should be done. See Chapter Seven for a discussion of the requirements in relation to service of orders.

Directions for hearing of contempt proceedings

47. CPR 81.7 gives the power to the court to make directions for the hearing, including ordering the attendance of witnesses and hearing oral evidence as it considers appropriate. There is a specific power to issue a bench warrant to secure the attendance of the defendant at both the directions and the substantive hearing.

Remedying breaches of CPR 81

48. The CPR 81 does not expressly give the court power to waive any procedural defect in the preparation or conduct of contempt proceedings. But the court has held that it retains such a power[137] . The overall test is whether the defendant, "*…having regard to the background against which the committal application is launched, would be in any doubt as to the substance of the breaches alleged*"- see paragraph 77 of the *Deutsche Bank* case.

49. The application notice "*needs to be clear enough to leave the respondent in no doubt as to the substance of the breaches at a point when he still has time to meet them*" [ibid para 79] although it need only "*set out a succinct summary, to be read in the light of the relevant background known to the parties; it is for the evidence to set out the detail*" [ibid para 80].

50. A schedule will be necessary in some cases, where there are many breaches, but is not essential [ibid, para 86].

51. Although breach of the requirements may well lead to sanctions, including even a strike out of the application, if a claimant can show that there has been "effective compliance" or a determined effort to comply, there is likely to be some leeway.

52. The case of *Business Mortgage Finance 4 plc v Hussain,*[138] is valuable background reading for applicants intending to pursue committal proceedings, and there is a useful summary of procedure and principles at paragraph 37-49. Essentially, the applicant is entitled to rely on CPR 3.1(2)(m) and 3.10.

---

[137] *Deutsche Bank AG v Sebastian Holdings Inc and anor* [2020] EWHC 3536 (Comm) at [148], a decision of Cockerill J

[138] [2022] EWHC 449 (Ch)

53. For instance, although personal service is mandatory, the court will dispense with it if sure that the defendant is evading service or aware of and fully informed about the contempt application. Although there are no absolute rules, the court should pay heed to the justice of what the particular circumstances require.

54. Equally, although there is no power to dispense with the requirement of a penal notice, the court was satisfied that it had this power and it could be exercised if it would occasion no injustice to the defendant.

55. At one stage in *Hussain*, the court issued a bench warrant with power to the Tipstaff and the police to be allowed to enter various properties using force if necessary.

56. The court also rejected the defendant's application to be heard remotely.

57. Preparation for a committal hearing is addressed in Chapter Thirteen.

CHAPTER TWELVE
ISSUE OF ARREST WARRANTS

KEY POINTS

1. Applications for a warrant under section 10 and CPR 65.46
2. Applications for warrants in respect of juveniles
3. Collecting evidence for the application
4. Test for the grant of a warrant
5. Preparing to execute the warrant
6. Arrest

Applications under section 10

1. When there is no power of arrest attached to a clause of the injunction, but a significant breach occurs, the Act allows a claimant to ask the court to issue a warrant of arrest without giving notice to the respondent. Under the old Act, a warrant could only be issued if a power of arrest could originally have been attached to the term of the injunction breached, but the new provision contains no such restriction, and nor does CPR 65.46.

2. The Act and the Rule set out the procedure, which is easy to follow.[139] First, in the same way as the test in relation to the

[139] Section 10, CPR 65.46, CPR PD 65.2 and CPR 23

imposition of a power of arrest, if the claimant "thinks" that the respondent is in breach, they may apply for the warrant.[140] Evidence must be substantiated on oath.

3. The application has to be made to the court which granted the injunction unless it was made in respect of a youth who has subsequently turned 18.[141] The procedure in CPR 23 must be used and the application is made without notice to a defendant, for obvious reasons. Care should be taken to prevent the Court serving a copy of the application on the defendant.

4. The warrant is issued in standard form, using an N602, which will be prepared by the court upon the application.

5. As an alternative to an application for a warrant, when there is no urgency, it is possible to apply to add a power of arrest to an existing provision.

Applications for warrants in respect of juveniles

6. Upon breach of the injunction by a juvenile, the applicant is entitled to apply to the Youth Court for a warrant of arrest.

7. But if the respondent has reached the age of 18 since the injunction was granted, proceedings should continue in the County Court. That will require the Youth Court to make an order transferring the proceedings.

8. Therefore if there is any danger of a breach as a defendant approaches the age of 18, as close to the defendant's birthday as possible to alert the Youth Court of the need to transfer the file.

---

[140] section 10 (1)

[141] section 10 (2)

Collecting evidence

9. Evidence of the breach needs to be provided to the court and can only be given by affidavit or orally.[142] If at all possible, it should be the affidavit of a victim personally, or if there isn't time to take one and get it sworn, a claimant employee or police officer etc. reporting the exact words of the victim.

10. Additionally, if the witnesses are unwilling to be named in an affidavit, detailed hearsay evidence should be sufficient to satisfy the test for the court. If it is possible to obtain any corroboration of the allegation, by CCTV, photograph of a weapon etc. it should be obtained and provided as an exhibit to the affidavit.

11. The test for a police officer tasked with an arrest is different to that of the court considering whether the breach is proved. So it's worth considering the subsequent breach proceedings and beginning to gather the evidence which will be needed to prove beyond reasonable doubt that the breach did occur. Such evidence gathering should not prevent the application for the warrant being made at the earliest possible stage, as it can be based on oral evidence.

12. If the application is made in such a hurry that only oral evidence is given, the CPR require the applicant to produce a written record of the evidence, which must then be served on the respondent when they are arrested.[143]

The test for the issue of a warrant

13. The court must be satisfied only that it has "reasonable grounds for believing" that the respondent has breached the injunction.[144]

---

[142] CPR 65.46 (2) and CPR PD 65.2 (1)

[143] CPR 65.46 (3)

[144] CPR PD 65.2 contains a prohibition on issue without proof of reasonable

This means that there is no need to satisfy the court that there has actually been a breach, only that there is reasonable evidence of a breach.

14. If a judge issues a warrant, they will do so on form N146. Care should be taken to ensure that it is fully and properly completed, and particularly that accurate details of the breaches are inserted, as the subsequent committal proceedings will only concern those breaches listed and for which the defendant was arrested.

15. If there has not been sufficient time to include in the application for the warrant all the other breaches, those allegations will need to be added to the committal application.

16. This can be done by a further arrest, by formal application to commit, or if the defendant agrees to have them dealt with in the same proceedings. This can be attractive to a defendant if they are threatened with facing subsequent further separate committal proceedings, which will have cost the applicant additional sums and the court extra time and may therefore put the defendant at risk of unsympathetic treatment from the court.

Preparing to execute the warrant

17. Once a warrant has been issued, it will be necessary to serve it on the police and then to ensure that it is executed as soon as possible. Often, either the respondent is also wanted on other grounds, or a particular officer is liaising with the applicant or responsible for dealing with the respondent and they go out to look for the respondent.

---

grounds

Arrest

18. Although there is a specific provision in section 9 requiring the police to bring the arrested person before the court within 24 hours, no such requirement appears in section 10 of the Act. Nothing in CPR 65.47 imposes the requirement.

19. In practice the police invariably bring the defendant to the County Court within those 24 hours. However, if there is more than 24 hours delay following arrest pursuant to a warrant, it is obviously arguable that committal proceedings can continue without the need to release the defendant and issue an application to commit.

20. As soon as an arrest takes place, the constable must inform the applicant.[145] It is also essential to inform the court to which the defendant will be brought.

21. See the Chapter Thirteen for procedure in the committal application.

---

[145] section 10 (7)

CHAPTER THIRTEEN PREPARATION FOR COMMITTALS, FIRST HEARINGS AND REMANDS

KEY POINTS

1. Planning for committal hearings
2. The right to silence
3. Proving Service of the Order
4. Dispensing with service
5. Service of Undertakings
6. Evidence of breach
7. Hearsay evidence in committals
8. Preparation
9. Procedure
10. The first (remand) hearing
11. Legal aid
12. Remands on bail or in custody

Planning for committal hearings

1. Once a defendant has been brought before the court, they must either be dealt with for the breach or remanded to another hearing. The outcome of the first hearing and the subsequent committal depends on so many variables it is not possible to plot a predictable course for these proceedings.

2. Some breaches of injunction can be dealt with immediately after arrest. Others end up involving a contested hearing on a single breach or a variety of allegations. All alleged contempts of court should be addressed swiftly and the court may need to be reminded of this imperative. Where a defendant is arrested and brought before the court, the contempt application must take place within 28 days. If proceeding by way of an application, the court might be reminded of the need to determine such applications without delay, especially when they relate to a breach of an injunction[146].

3. The pre-2020 rules mandated that committal hearings would not generally be heard less than 14 days after service of the application. Although the rule has not been replicated in the new CPR 81, the rationale remains. Defendants should be given sufficient time to instruct solicitors, seek funding and obtain evidence upon which they would wish to rely, so they can properly advance their case.

4. But if a defendant was given an adjournment to allow him to obtain legal representation, "*the court may refuse to grant further adjournments for the same purpose where to do so would not be in the interests of justice and may unduly prejudiced the claimant for the committal order*" [see the *Double Negative v Mortlette* case]

---

[146] see particularly the case of *Double Negative Ltd v Mortelette* [2018] EWHC 1811 (QB), cited in the White Book 2022 at CPR81.7.1

5. Thus there will often be a conflict between the need to allow a defendant time and the 28 day limit.

The right to silence

6. At every stage of a committal, it is important to bear in mind the right to silence, but also that it is not absolute. An admission made when a defendant has not been cautioned may not be admissible against them.

7. On arrest the police will almost certainly give a defendant the standard caution and repeat it if they interview them. Subsequently it should not be forgotten during the preparation of the committal.

8. That right is qualified by the same restrictions as apply to criminal defendants. There is much case law on the subject. An applicant should start from the basis that the defendant must be clearly informed of his right not to say anything. They should also be warned that, if they remain silent in circumstances which clearly call for an explanation, silence can be taken into account in assessing the persuasiveness of the evidence adduced by the applicant.[147]

9. At the hearing the applicant and the court need to ensure that they do not effectively force the respondent to give evidence. During the hearing the court should remind a defendant of their qualified right to silence and in appropriate cases, the right not to incriminate themselves.

---

[147] *Murray v UK* [1996] ECHR 18731/91 at paragraph 47, cited in *Khawaja v Popat and Popat* [2016] EWCA Civ 362 at para 30. See also the. See also *Business Mortgage Finance 4 plc and others v Hussain* [2022] All ER (D) 53 (Mar) [2022] EWHC 449 (Ch), paragraph 41

10. It is essential to bear in mind that, even if a respondent serves and files evidence in response to a contempt application, they are under no obligation to rely on it and it is not to be taken as having been adduced in evidence. Of course this does not stop the applicant from gathering evidence in preparation of any reply to what is said in the written evidence.

11. Contempt proceedings should not be heard at the same time as other applications involving the lower, civil standard of proof, in which a party is obliged to respond to the other party's case.[148]

12. There is no reason why those hearings cannot take place consecutively, particularly where an application to vary an injunction order is made at the same time as committal proceedings are taking place.

13. Equally, an application for possession of a property can be heard immediately after the committal. It is rarely logical to deal with allegations which are the subject of forthcoming committal proceedings in a civil hearing before the committal is heard.

Proving Service of the Order

14. CPR 81.5 specifically provides that the judgement or order cannot be enforced by committal unless service has been proved or pursuant to an order for alternative service or dispensation with service under 81.5 (1) and CPR 6.27 or 28 (see below), so the court will check that the order was properly served.

15. Before allowing an arrest to take place or applying to commit for contempt the applicant should confirm that there is good evidence of service. The applicant should check that the order served is the same one it seeks to enforce.

---

148 *In the matter of L (A Child) and Gous Oddin* [2016] EWCA Civ 173 at para 29-43

16. The right to silence means that a defendant will not have to admit that they have been served, so formal proof, either from the court record or from the applicant must be adduced. In the absence of such proof, it is possible that a defendant might avoid committal.

17. Under the new rules, if the defendant has a solicitor on the record, service can be effected on them and will be approved by the court unless the representative objects in writing within seven days of receipt of the application and evidence[149].

18. If there is no objection, the solicitor must provide to the defendant at once a copy of the application and evidence and "*take all reasonable steps to ensure the defendant understands them*". If they object to service on them, a judge must consider the parties' representations and decide what to do on the papers, unless the Judge directs that a hearing should take place.

19. The new committal application form also requires significant detail to be given of the circumstances of service of the original injunction, so there should be no chance that an application is made prior to service being effective properly. Of course if service of the original order had not been effective when the breach occurred, the court cannot commit for that breach.

Dispensing with service/authorising service by an alternative means

20. A number of points on service are commonly encountered at enforcement stage. Defendants may:

- refuse to accept that they have been served because they have not taken the papers from the process server;

[149] CPR 81.5(2)

- claim that it was not them who accepted the papers-but a relative or friend;

- evade the process server and, if they are not a professional who knows how to serve, the documents are merely left in a post-box or similar;

- claim that they are unable to read or otherwise had some reason why they could not understand the proceedings, or that the papers were destroyed by someone or something else.

21. CPR 81.5 and CPR 6.25 & 6.27-28 give the court specific power to approve service by an alternative method or dispense with personal service of the judgement or order and of the committal application.

22. These are important provisions. They allow for *retrospective* dispensation with service, as well as an *anticipatory* order providing that the claimant can serve by an alternative means. As well as the methods listed above this could include telling the defendant orally, service by text, or private message on Facebook or other social media, by serving or even, e.g., telling a partner or relative.

23. If the court is satisfied that the defendant has evaded service, it can retrospectively dispense with personal service, but it is obviously better to obtain an order at the time confirming that the court is satisfied that the order came to the attention of the defendant, or even that he was aware of an intention to bring it to his notice but deliberately avoided service.

Service of Undertakings

24. Undertakings are always given personally to the court and as a result, the provisions in relation to service are different. The court

should serve by handing a copy of the undertaking to the defendant before they leave the court building, by posting it to them at their home address or place of business, or to their solicitor.

25. Alternatively, if service cannot be effected in one of those ways, the court officer will deliver to the claimant, who must then serve it personally on the defendant as soon as practicable.

Evidence of breach

26. Following arrest, it is necessary to consider whether to collect further evidence of the breach or of other breaches, particularly because the burden of proof is higher, it being necessary to prove allegations beyond reasonable doubt.

Circumstantial evidence in committals

27. The judge in *Business Mortgage Finance 4 plc v Hussain*[150] found multiple contempts proved, substantially on the basis of circumstantial evidence of breach, which can be used if the court is "*satisfied that the facts are inconsistent with any conclusion other than that the contempt in question has been committed.*"

28. Further: "*The court need not be sure on every item of evidence which takes into account in concluding that a contempt has been established. It must however be sure of any intermediate fact which is either an essential element of, or a necessary step on the way towards, such a conclusion.*"[151]

---

[150] [2022] EWHC 449 (Ch)

[151] *Shepherd v The Queen* 170 CLR 573 (High Court of Australia)

Hearsay evidence in committals

29. Hearsay evidence is admissible in contempt proceedings,[152] so a claimant should not be dissuaded from pursuing a committal simply because a witness will not or cannot come to give live evidence.[153] Ideally that hearsay will not take the form of anonymous allegations reported only by another witness for the applicant, although that evidence should be corroborated in the best means possible.

30. It may be possible to persuade a witness to provide an affidavit on the condition that their name and address is withheld from the court. It may nevertheless be possible to identify them from what they say, so degree of care is necessary in the preparation of such evidence.

31. Uncorroborated hearsay is not likely to persuade a court to make a finding of contempt when it is the only evidence against a defendant who is prepared to get into the witness box and contradict it. A defendant can rely on what was said about hearsay in *Moat Housing*, so a claimant must prove in evidence the veracity of the hearsay evidence, particularly by presenting some oral or other evidence and relying on the hearsay as corroboration.

32. However, there are many circumstances in which hearsay evidence may form a central plank of a claimant's case. It may be adduced as the main evidence against a defendant, but corroborated by other material.

---

[152] *Wear Valley District Council v Robson* [2008] EWCA Civ 1470 at para 9-10

[153] see also *Circle Housing Old Ford v Claire Robinson* (2015) 2 September, unrep., at para 4

Alternatives to anonymous hearsay evidence

33. There are some options available to a claimant which is struggling to persuade a witness to be named and to attend court.

Witness summonses

34. Witnesses can be encouraged to give evidence by taking away their ability to refuse to attend. Paradoxically, if they are able to say to a defendant that they have no choice but to come to court and give evidence, their initial reluctance to do so may evaporate

35. CPR 34 contains the relevant provisions and care must be taken to comply, as the witness can object to a defective summons, e.g. because the 'conduct money' is not paid, or it is served less than 7 days before the hearing. CPR 34.5 (2) allows the court to provide for short service when the application for the summons is made.

Depositions

36. A party can also apply to have a witness examined before a trial,[154] before a judge, an examiner of the court or 'such other person as the court appoints', who can be a barrister or solicitor. This might be particularly useful if a witness is willing to give evidence but unable to do so, e.g. because they are in hospital or otherwise unable to get to court.

Other witness protection measures

37. All the other ways in which witnesses can be protected can also be considered. Often a witness will be reassured merely by the presence of a screen preventing a defendant from looking at them while they are giving evidence.

[154] CPR 34.8-15

38. It can be helpful to familiarise a witness with the court room by bringing them to an interim hearing. If this is done on a without-notice hearing there will be no danger that the defendant will be present at court and so no issue as to intimidation by their mere presence.

Preparation for the committal hearing

Hearing Bundles

39. It is important to prepare a paginated, indexed bundle in all but the simplest of cases: it is much easier to present the application if the judge and the defendant can be referred to evidence by page and paragraph number, and the judge will find it easier to read the papers and make notes before the hearing. That bundle will contain material additional to the one prepared for any interim or final hearing.

Additional content of the bundle

40. The bundle should contain the version of the injunction originally sought, that which is in force and a draft of any order sought by way of variation as a result of the contempt proceedings. The affidavits relied on in support of the contempt proceedings, and any additional evidence filed by the defendant should be contained in a section separate to the evidence adduced in earlier hearings.

Procedure

41. The committal hearing is governed by CPR 81.8 and an applicant must ensure that there is substantial compliance with the rules.

42. Non-compliance is not necessarily fatal to an application. A respondent must show some real detriment to them caused by a defect in procedure and the court will overlook errors which do

not cause any significant prejudice to the respondent (see *Deutsche Bank AG v Sebastian Holdings Inc and anor* and *Business Mortgage Finance v Hussain*, above).

43. Errors in committal proceedings may give rise to grounds for an application to dismiss them and accordingly any defendant who finds procedural or other errors should rely on them to support a submission.

44. Previously the Practice Direction to CPR 81 gave the court a specific power to strike out a committal application, but only if it appeared that on the application and evidence it disclosed no reasonable ground for making the allegations, it was an abuse of process or otherwise likely to obstruct the just disposal of existing proceedings, or if there had been a failure to comply with a rule, practice direction or court order. The court retains that inherent jurisdiction, which would be exercised under CPR 2.3 (1) and CPR 3.1 (2) (m).

45. In *Nicholls*[155] Lord Woolf said:

> "*As long as the order made by the judge was a valid order, the approach of this Court will be to uphold the order in the absence of any prejudice or injustice to the contemnor as a consequence of doing so.*"

46. But there are various examples in other areas of law where committal applications have been held to be an abuse of process or for some other reason amenable to strike out. If the reason for the contempt application is a failure to comply with a court order, any application to strike out is less likely to succeed[156].

---

155 *Nicholls v Nicholls* [1997] 2 All ER 97

156 *Absolute Living Developments Ltd v DS7 Ltd and Ors* [2018] EWHC 1717 (Ch) at para 36

47. CPR 81.8 contains provisions about hearings in contempt proceedings, and you should note that there is a requirement that advocates and the judge must be robed in all hearings, whether or not the court sits in public. However, sometimes judges will not wish to be robed and advocates should follow suit.

48. The court will sit in public unless it otherwise directs, irrespective of the parties' consent.

The first (remand) hearing

49. Unless the defendant wishes to admit the contempt and apply to purge it immediately upon their first appearance, the court is unlikely to deal with the breach at the initial hearing.

50. Practice differs between adult courts as to whether arrests are dealt with in courtrooms with a dock (Crown or Magistrates') or in the normal County Court hearing room. A defendant will be brought up from the cells and placed in the dock or in the well of the court. If the hearing is listed in a standard County Courtroom, the defendant may remain handcuffed or not depending on the degree of perceived risk.

51. When the case is called on, the claimant's representative should ensure that the judge has all the relevant papers if possible, being the injunction file and the documents produced immediately before and after arrest. The defendant must be reminded of their right to silence but then (unless they insist on speaking to a solicitor first) asked if they are prepared to admit the contempt or not. If the contempt is admitted, sentence can be dealt with there and then (see below).

52. Committal proceedings should not be adjourned to await the outcome of criminal proceedings in normal circumstances.[157]

[157] *Lomas v Parle* [2003] EWCA Civ 1804, [2004] 1 WLR 1642; at paragraph 49, cited in *Birmingham City Council v Thomas Gill* [2016] EWCA Civ

> "*Contempt proceedings should be dealt with swiftly and decisively... They should be adjourned to await the outcome of the criminal trial only where there was a risk of serious prejudice which might lead to injustice*".[158]

Legal aid

53. The defendant can rely on regulation 9(v) of the Criminal Legal Aid (General) Regulations 2013, SI 2013/9, which says:

> *"The following proceedings are criminal proceedings for the purposes of section 14(h) of the [Legal Aid, Sentencing and Punishment of Offenders Act 2012] (criminal proceedings) –*
>
> *(v) any other proceedings that involve the determination of a criminal charge for the purposes of Article 6(1) of the European Convention on Human Rights."*

54. Many defendants do not take advantage of their right to free legal advice and they or the court will hesitate to have the contempt dealt with at the first hearing. If the defendant has had an opportunity to take legal advice, the hearing is likely to be disposed of more efficiently.

55. When the Pre-Action Protocol comes into force it will be mandatory to inform defendants of their right to legal aid from the outset.

---

608 at paragraph 19

[158] *Magdouch v Zakaria Rmiki* 29 July 1999, unrep., cited in *Leicester City Council v Lewis* and see the White Book, CPR 81.7.1 and Vol 2, para 3C-25

56. Solicitors do not have to hold a criminal or civil legal aid contract, they can apply for an individual case contract ("ICC")[159] The guidance was updated in June 2022.

57. Applications can be made online through the portal or on paper. There is no means testing and the interests of justice test is met by the nature of the contempt proceedings and the existence of one or more of nine possible reasons. The instruction of Counsel is automatically included in the order. There is a limit of £1368.75 but applications to extend can be made by email to the LAB.

58. CPR 81.4 (2) (i) and (j) require the committal application to include statements that the defendant has a right to be legally represented and to have a reasonable opportunity to get that representation and apply for legal aid without any means test.

59. If a defendant wants legal representation the court is obliged to make sure it is available.[160] Lack of legal representation in committal proceedings is a serious procedural flaw[161], although a defendant may choose not to be represented. Such a refusal should be fully noted before the court proceeds, and should form part of the recital on any order.

Remands on bail or in custody and directions

60. The court has power to release a defendant subject to a recognizance or other conditions to be complied with before or after release, or to remand them in custody.

---

[159] https://assets.publishing.service.gov.uk/government/uploads/system/uploads/attachment_data/file/620018/civil-contempt-guidance.pdf

[160] *Re O (Committal): Legal Representation* [2019] 4 WLR 140 at para 2

[161] *Brown v Haringey LBC* [2017] 1 WLR 542

61. Any remand must be for a period of eight days (or three clear days if remanded to the custody of a police constable[162]) unless it remands for a medical examination and report under paragraph 5 or 6 of the Schedule, or if remanding on bail, both parties' consent.[163] However, both parties can consent to a longer period.

62. The County Court judge has power to impose conditions on the grant of bail, either by (1) taking a recognizance[164] or (2) by requiring the defendant to comply (before release on bail or later) with any requirements which "*appear to the court to be necessary to secure that the person does not interfere with witnesses or otherwise obstruct the course of justice.*"[165]

63. Such conditions might prevent a defendant from communicating with victims, or even from returning to a particular area, including their home, or require them to live e.g. at a bail hostel or with a relative.

64. If there is any fear that witnesses will be interfered with, the defendant will carry on breaching the injunction or fail to attend the next hearing, the claimant can make submissions in relation to bail.

65. It will be necessary to consider whether neighbours will be safe if the defendant is allowed back to their home address, whether there is another address available for them, the possibility of additional prohibitions or requirements on the injunction, e.g. an limited or full exclusion or curfew, an additional power of arrest. If there is sufficient time before the hearing, a witness

---

[162] para 4 of Schedule 1

[163] Section 11 (5) and Schedule 1. Note that any magistrate remanding a youth must ensure that the committal takes place before the Youth Court which granted the injunction (section 11 (6)).

[164] under paragraph 2 and 8 of Schedule 1

[165] para 9 of Schedule 1

statement should be prepared, setting out what the concerns are and how they should be addressed.

66. Such evidence can be presented to the court as hearsay, from the case officer, for example in the form of emails or records of telephone conversations, or in material provided to the police.

67. The court should be provided with a copy of the defendant's criminal antecedents, which may well be helpful in the decision whether to grant bail.

68. The decision whether to remand in custody can prove pivotal to a defendant who is considering denying the contempt. A defendant remanded in custody who has not been convicted receives privileges which experienced defendants will seek to exploit if they believe a custodial sentence is inevitable for the contempt. They may therefore prefer to be remanded in custody.

69. It is mandatory to remind a defendant of their right to silence and this can result in a decision not to say anything, however strong the evidence against them, unless they are represented. A defendant should also be told that if they choose not to say anything, adverse comment may be made if it later transpires that they rely on facts which could have been mentioned at the time.

70. There may also be some advantage in reminding a defendant either before or during the hearing that the court may take a different view of sentence if it does not hear the full facts straight from the mouth of a witness. This can be done either by the court or by the claimant's representative.

71. There is also a significant discount due to any defendant who admits a breach early. As in criminal proceedings, early admissions are reflected by lower sentences. In the interests of fairness to defendants, this should be pointed out at the first hearing, particularly if they are unrepresented. This will prevent any later injustice to them in sentencing.

72. If a defendant maintains their right to silence, it is important to have the matter listed for a contested committal hearing immediately, so as to avoid running into difficulties with the 28-day time limit.

73. There is no automatic sanction for a breach of bail under the 2014 Act – it is not a criminal offence and nor is it a contempt of court unless the judge adds to the injunction further terms, which can and should carry a power of arrest if they are to be enforceable by the police. The CJC report recommends that the Civil Rules Procedure Committee should consider whether PD 65 should be amended to clarify these matters.

74. Some judges will wish to adjourn briefly (e.g. for a week) to allow a defendant to seek legal advice and attend for a 'plea and directions' hearing. That is sensible, provided that at that first hearing the court fixes the date for the final hearing in any event.

75. The claimant then must decide what evidence will be needed to prove the contempt and therefore how long a hearing will be, and to agree with the judge and the defendant on some suitable directions. If possible, a defendant should be encouraged to file a witness statement in reply, although there is no obligation on them to give any advance notice of their defence.

76. If a defendant has been arrested for more than one contempt, it is often helpful for the claimant to prepare a 'Scott Schedule' setting out the date, substance of the allegations, the location of the evidence and the paragraph of the injunction alleged to be breached, leaving space for comments by the defendant and the judge.

Remands for medical reports

77. Medical reports can be ordered by the judge if there is "reason to think" that one will be needed, in which case an adult can be

remanded in custody for not more than three weeks at a time, or on bail for not more than four weeks at a time.

78. Additionally, if the court is satisfied on the evidence of a doctor that there is "reason to suspect" the defendant is suffering from mental disorder and that doctor is "of the opinion" that it would be impracticable for the report on the defendant's mental condition to be made if they were remanded on bail, the court can remand the defendant to a hospital or registered establishment specified by it.[166] Given the shortage of such beds, these orders are unlikely to be made except in the most serious of cases.

Further remands

79. The Schedule also allows for further remands in the absence of the defendant in limited circumstances; if the court is satisfied that they are unable because of illness or accident to appear or to be brought before the court, para 4 of the Schedule applies, when they can be remanded for more than 8 (or 3) days in custody.[167]

[166] para 6 of Schedule 1

[167] under paragraph 7

CHAPTER FOURTEEN COMMITTAL HEARINGS AND SENTENCING

KEY POINTS

1. The committal hearing
2. Proving the breach
3. The right to silence
4. Findings of breach
5. Sentence following a finding of breach
6. Applications to purge contempt
7. Disability Discrimination at the point of sentence
8. Sentencing under 18-year-olds
9. Breach not proved

The committal hearing

1. The hearing should take place in front of a District Judge, who is given express jurisdiction to deal with committals.

2. Some County Courts choose to list committals in front of Circuit Judges or Recorders. Provided that they are familiar with antisocial behaviour law, there is no harm in this, although it does limit the avenues of appeal.

3. The hearing must be in open court and the judge should wear robes, as should barristers and solicitors appearing in court.

4. The defendant will be brought from custody into the court room. If the case has been listed in a magistrates' or Crown Court, there will be a dock. Otherwise, they will sit, sometimes in handcuffs, in the well of the court.

5. The case must be called on and the defendant must be identified. The judge should then ask the claimant to explain the circumstances of the arrest. The defendant should be reminded of their right to silence and, if they do not have legal representation, asked whether they wish to instruct a lawyer.

6. Provided the defendant is either represented or agrees to proceed without a lawyer, they can be asked whether they admit the alleged contempt of court.

7. If they are content to proceed with the hearing, the defendant may either admit the contempt in full, or make partial admissions/deny it entirely, and require a claimant to prove some or all of the breaches.

Proving the breach

8. As the penalty involves an interference with the liberty of the subject, the power is exercised with care and only in cases where disobedience is intentional and in all the circumstances a committal order as appropriate.[168] *Broomleigh* is worthy of attention, particularly on this point as it is necessary to ensure that the judge in a committal gives a reasoned and full judgement to reduce the chances the findings that it will be successfully appealed.[169]

---

[168] *Broomleigh Housing Association Ltd v Okonkwo* [2010] EWCA Civ 1113

[169] at paragraph 23 in the appeal the court was dealing with proof of the

9. The failure to obey a court order depends on all the relevant facts and circumstances-is not automatically a contempt.[170]

10. The applicant must prove the contempt as follows: "*(a) having received notice of the order the contemnor did an act prohibited by the order or failed to do an act required by the order within the time set by the order; (b) he intended to do the act or failed to do the act as the case may be; (c) he had knowledge of all the facts which would make the carrying out of the prohibited act or the omission to do the required act a breach of the order. The act constituting the breach must be deliberate rather than merely inadvertent, but an intention to commit a breach is not necessary, although intention or lack of intention to flout the court's order is relevant to penalty.*"[171]

11. Issues of motive and belief or lack of it that the contender is acting in breach of the Order are irrelevant.[172] To put it another way, although it is not necessary to show a wilful intention to disobey a court order, the applicant has to show an intention to do a prohibited act knowing the consequences. This is particularly important in contempt proceedings against individuals with a mental disability.[173]

12. That first point is essential – there is no point in proceeding with a committal application if it cannot be proved that the respondent has been served with the order or that he knew of its terms because he was in court when it was made. Then sufficient

grounds for contempt and described the findings of the first instance Judge as amounting to nothing more than "perfunctory consideration" of the facts.

[170] *AB and CD Re Nobile Officium* [2015] ScotCS CSIH_25 at para 29

[171] *F W Farnsworth v Lacy and Ors* [2012] EWHC 2830 (Ch)

[172] *Hewlett Packard Enterprise Co v Sage* at paragraph 16

[173] *P v P (Contempt of Court: Mental Capacity)* [1999] 2 F.L.R.

evidence must be put before the court to satisfy the criminal standard of proof of the breach.

13. The second and third hurdles need to be considered separately, as many defendants put forward alternative interpretations of the terms of an order. For example, an exclusion order worded "*Not to enter Parsons Close at any time after 4 PM on 31 May 2019*" is arguably enforceable only until midnight on the day. The sentence should continue, e.g. "*... until further order of the court or (the expiry date of the injunction), whichever is the sooner.*" It may be possible to prove that a defendant was in court and was well aware that the injunction applied after midnight, but that still might not save the committal.

14. If a defendant has denied any breaches, the court will proceed with a trial in the usual way. Evidence must be given, either from the witness box and/or in hearsay form. As judges prefer to hear the evidence of a live witness to reading an affidavit, it is important to secure their attendance if possible. A witness summons may be issued in respect of any reluctant individual. Proper procedures must be observed, including payment of the correct recompense for their travel expenses.

15. The burden of proof remains throughout on the applicant, who must prove each allegation of contempt of court through breach of the injunction beyond any reasonable doubt. To gain an idea of the type of evidence which will not suffice to persuade a judge to the requisite standard, it is instructive to look at County Court decisions on committals.[174]

---

[174] *Dudley Metropolitan Borough Council v Shaun Hill* [2018] EWCOP 35

The right to silence

16. The defendant is not obliged to give evidence and must be warned of their right to silence before giving evidence. There is a separate right not to incriminate oneself in the witness box.

17. In criminal cases statutory restrictions have been placed on the right to silence, which are likely to be of assistance in a committal: the defendant retains his right to silence to the extent he is not under any absolute duty to say anything, either under interrogation or at the hearing.

18. However, in both criminal and civil courts "proper" inferences may be drawn from (1) a failure by a defendant to give evidence, or a failure without good reason to answer any question at the hearing, (2) a failure to mention certain facts when questioned after being cautioned, (3) failing to account for any objects, substances or marks or (4) the defendant's presence in a particular place.

19. If an issue arises as to a defendant relying on his right to silence, reference should be made to a textbook on evidence, e.g. *Phipson*, as there is much case law on the issue.

Findings of breach

20. If the court finds any contempt proved, it must move on to consider whether to make any penalty for the proven breach of the court order and, if so, whether that should take the form of committal to prison, a fine or sequestration of assets.

21. Findings of breach must now be recorded on an "Order on determination of proceedings for contempt of court" form N603, issued under CPR 81.9 (1).

22. The breaches found proved should be recorded on the N603, which the court will prepare, probably with the assistance of the

advocate. The order will need to provide various details in respect of the hearing and should generally be completed in consultation with the advocates.

23. Publication of a transcript of the judgment where a sentence of imprisonment is passed: In *Lovett v Wigan BC* (para 29) the Court of Appeal stressed the importance of CPR 81.8 (8). The purpose of the requirement is to facilitate legal advice relating to appeals. The court said that judges "*must plainly undertake its responsibility in a timely fashion, and take heed of a request from a defendant wishing to appeal*" but a breach of that duty is not a ground of appeal.

Sentence following a finding of breach

24. Before sentencing the contemnor, even after a trial of the breach allegations the court should ask the defendant whether they have anything to say by way of apology or explanation before any penalty is imposed for the contempt.

25. That penalty may take the form of imprisonment, a fine or 'sequestration of assets'. In antisocial behaviour proceedings the latter two are rarely relevant. Additionally, the court can make no order, possibly save in relation to costs.

26. As mentioned above, guidance on sentencing, both in respect of procedure and principles has now been given by the Court of Appeal in *Christopher Lovett v Wigan Borough Council.*[175] this judgment should now be read and referred to by all involved in any sentencing contempt hearing.

27. In *Amicus Horizon Ltd v Thorley*[176] the Court of Appeal had said that the Sentencing Guidelines Council's Definitive Guidelines

[175] [2022] EWCA Civ 1631

[176] *Amicus Horizon Ltd v Thorley* [2012] EWCA Civ 817

for breaches of antisocial behaviour orders[177] were pertinent in antisocial behaviour order sentencing. In *Lovett* [at 36] the court disapproved of this approach, for the reasons given in paragraphs 32-4 of the judgment.

28. Save in special circumstances, e.g. when the breach is a criminal offence itself, it said that the guidelines are relevant only in "*the very broadest and generalised sense*". As a general rule if the sentence contemplated by the County Court is the same or more severe than that suggested in the guidelines, it is likely to be wrong.

29. They referred with approval [at para 32] to the judgment in *Hale v Tanner.*[178] That case made the important point that there is a distinction between the principles relating to criminal sentencing and those applicable to contempt of court, because the circumstances in contempt cases are more various and the powers of the civil court on more limited.

30. But a key difference is the objectives underlying penalties for contempt are different from those in crime, particularly in relation to ensuring future compliance with the order. The court mentioned various cases stressing the importance of this aspect (at para 33-4) and pointed out that the CJC report, which could be understood as putting the objective of punishment first[179], was wrong to do so.

31. In *Lovett v Wigan* the court also referred with approval to the 10 general points in *Hale v Tanner.*

[177] now replaced by the updated "Breach Offences Definitive Guideline" which still do not explicitly refer to civil injunctions but can be taken as applying to them on the same reasoning as used in *"Amicus v Thorley"*.

[178] *Hale v Tanner* [2000] 1 WLR 2377 at para 26-36

[179] at paragraph 383 of the report

32. The court considered the objectives of sentencing [39], being ensuring future compliance with the order, punishment and rehabilitation. It listed the disposals available [40-42]. It said that there is a custody threshold (43] and "*custody should be reserved for the most serious breaches, and for less serious cases where other methods of securing compliance with the order have failed.*"

33. Suspension of sentences was addressed [45], the court saying that the alternative is to adjourn consideration of sentence, which "*the court can use as an opportunity to speak directly to the contemnor about their behaviour*".

34. The new sentencing grid envisages adjourning consideration of sentence in all but the most serious cases. This is likely to replace the imposition of a suspended sentence in most cases.

35. It is likely to be appropriate to indicate what sentence would have been imposed if the matter had not been adjourned, and state clearly the consequences of good or bad conduct pending the sentencing hearing, preferably by a recital to the order.

36. If on sentencing after an adjournment there is no evidence of breaches or other relevant bad conduct, "*the ultimate sentence should usually be a lesser sentence than would be imposed if the case had not been adjourned. In some cases the court may conclude that a final will be sufficient.*" But as most defendants are impecunious, this is likely to be of limited relevance in most cases.

37. Otherwise, in deciding on sentence, the degree of harm and culpability are relevant and the court referred to the CJC report, Annex 1, which proposes a sentencing grid based on the Sentencing Council's guidelines. The court provided guidance to which reference must be made in every committal sentencing hearing [46-56].

38. The court also said that in the *most minor* cases it may be appropriate to make no order if the impact of the proceedings is

likely to achieve the purposes of the contempt jurisdiction. This should involve an investigation whether the defendant is genuinely remorseful and whether there a reasonable expectation of compliance.

39. The court should impose a penalty for each breach found proved (rather than just for a single breach leaving the rest with no penalty) and terms of imprisonment can be concurrent or consecutive, with due regard to totality. Custody should never be imposed if an alternative course is sufficient and appropriate, and it should be the shortest term which will achieve the purpose for which it is being imposed.

40. Familiarity with older cases concerning sentencing is important to provide context to anyone committal sentencing .180 For a helpful example of the application of sentencing authorities pre-*Lovett v Wigan BC*, see *Wigan BC v Elizabeth Elliot.181* That report also gives a flavour of the rollercoaster ride possible in any committal hearing.

41. Time spent in custody on remand pending the committal hearing is not automatically deducted from the sentence, so the court will need to carry out a careful calculation of the appropriate sentence after deduction of the days on remand. As prisoners should serve only half the sentence which is imposed, that time on remand must be doubled before deduction from the total sentence.

[180] see for instance *Gill v Birmingham City Council* [2016] EWCA Civ 608, *Leicester City Council v Alvin Spencer Lewis* (2001) 33 H.L.R. 37, where the judge imprisoned the defendant for six months for a single breach, and, at the opposite end of the scale, *Chief Constable of Surrey Police v Levi Stevens* (2019) 12 March, unrep., where the judge gave the defendant a 4 week sentence, suspended from 26 February to 31 March 2019 – only 33 days.

[181] Available on *Wigan Borough Council v Elliott* [2019] EW Misc 4(CC)

42. Care needs to be taken to complete the N603 and (in the event of an immediate sentence of imprisonment) N604 forms properly.

43. In respect of the N603, this means completing each section and striking through those which do not apply, recording what evidence was read/heard, inserting full particulars of the breaches found proved (or attaching a schedule) and the sentence imposed in respect of each, the order for costs and recording how service of the original injunction was proved and how the proceedings were progressed (i.e. by arrest or otherwise).

44. The N604 is more straightforward, but equally fundamental. It is suggested that the box specifying the period of custody imposed is completed in terms of weeks or days so that there can be no mistake as to the length of the sentence imposed.

45. A judge hearing a committal application is obliged to send a copy of their judgement to the Ministry of Justice if they find any contempt proved. The court will order a transcript of their sentencing remarks, which can be found on the judicial website.[182] Some judges may need to be reminded of the requirement to do so. However breach of the requirement is not a ground of appeal against sentence[183].

Disability Discrimination at the point of sentence

46. It is rare to see disability discrimination raised only at the sentencing stage of committal proceedings following breach. Usually, the arguments will have been addressed as part of the consideration whether an injunction should be imposed in the first place, or upon arrest if the court believes there is a mental

---

[182] https://www.judiciary.uk/ , although the search facility does not work well

[183] *Lovett v Wigan BC,* para 68-9

health issue. However occasionally an individual is not represented until they come to be sentenced.

47. Care should be taken to address properly all issues of mental welfare prior to proceeding with a committal when the applicant has reason to believe there may be issues either as to capacity or psychiatric illness.

48. For instance, in a case[184] where the defendant had applied for permission to appeal a welfare determination in Court of Protection proceedings and the court decided to carry on with a committal application against her before determination of the permission application, the Court of Appeal was critical of the decision. There is clearly a balance to be drawn given the urgency of all committal proceedings.

49. But if the applicant was not aware of any disability, and so has not previously carried out any PSED enquiry then the court is entitled to take that into account. See the discussion of *Taylor v Slough Borough Council*, in Chapter Five.

Applications to discharge contempt

50. At any time after sentence has been imposed and a defendant committed to prison, they can apply to the court to be released, using the CPR 23 procedure.[185] Properly put, this is an application to "discharge the contempt". The contemnor must be offered the opportunity to 'discharge their contempt' if they request it while in custody. They can also appeal without permission against a committal order which results in imprisonment, relying on CPR 52.3 (1) (i).

[184] *Devon County Council v Teresa Kirk* [2016] EWCA Civ 1221

[185] the procedural requirements are contained in CPR 81.10

51. In an application to purge, the contemnor will direct their efforts toward getting immediate release, or at least deferred release at a future date earlier than they would otherwise be freed from the sentence. They must satisfy the judge that they are genuinely apologetic and that there will be no further contempt of court. An applicant asking to discharge their contempt will need to satisfy the court of genuine contrition, along with a number of other matters set out by Wilson LJ in a Court of Appeal case.[186]

52. On an application to purge the court cannot vary the sentence so as to suspend the unexpired term of the sentence. In the application the court will also "*consider afresh the sentence imposed with a view to deciding afresh whether it is absolutely necessary that the contemnor serve the remainder of the unexpired term*".[187]

52. The court is entitled to find, even on the basis of a letter from a defendant and without hearing any oral evidence, that they have purged their contempt and to order their release from custody after serving a portion of their sentence.[188] Only the contemnor can appeal without permission against a committal order. A claimant can appeal against a sentence which it considers to be unduly lenient, although they will require permission to do so.

Sentencing under 18-year-olds

53. A defendant who is under 18 will have been remanded to appear before the Youth Court which granted the injunction[189].

54. In the youth court a supervision order can be imposed or the court can order detention in youth custody, a secure training centre or secure accommodation for up to three months.

---

[186] *CJ v Flintshire Borough Council* [2010] EWCA Civ393

[187] *Balli, Re Contempt of Court Act 1981* (No. 2) at paras 16 and 23

[188] *Poole BC v Hambridge* [2007] EWCA Civ 990, unrep

[189] by section 9 (6)

Supervision orders are made under Part 2 of Schedule 2 and can comprise:

- a supervision requirement;
- an activity or curfew requirement. Curfew requirements can be enforced by electronic tagging.

55. If the court is considering imposing a supervision order, it needs to follow the process in paragraph 2 of Part 2. The maximum term of any supervision order is six months.

56. Activity requirements can require the youth to participate in activities, either for short periods or on a residential basis, for not less than 12 or more than 24 days.

57. A curfew must require the defaulter to remain at a specified place for periods of not less than two but no more than eight hours in any one day. Therefore youths cannot be required to stay at home during the whole of the evening and night.

58. If a supervision order is breached a youth court can then impose custody. The original supervision order can be revoked and replaced by a detention order. The court can also impose a new supervision order.

Detention orders

59. Part 3 of Schedule 2 of the Act contains the power to impose a custodial term on a "defaulter" and the Schedule is essential reading for anyone dealing with youth injunction orders.

60. Unlike the adult court, a youth court is severely restricted in the imposition of any custodial penalty. It has to find that the severity or extent of the behaviour constituting contempt warrants detention and that no other penalty is appropriate. It also needs to be satisfied expressly and beyond reasonable doubt

that the defendant has breached the injunction without any reasonable excuse.

61. Additionally, the Youth Offending Team needs to be consulted and any representations they make taken into account. The maximum sentence is only three months and can only be imposed in respect of those aged 14 or over.[190]

62. For this reason, if possible injunction proceedings should be taken against the parent or carer if possible, requiring them to exercise control over the youth concerned.

63. If a defaulter reaches the age of 18 during the sentencing process, a new supervision order or a detention order cannot be made against them.

Revocation of the detention order

64. In the same way that a perpetrator can apply to purge their contempt even after the imposition of a custodial sentence, a juvenile can (after consulting the YOT) apply under paragraph 15 of Part 3 to revoke the detention order. The court has a discretion to revoke, depending on "circumstances that have arisen since the detention order was made" which "include the conduct of the defaulter."

65. If such an application is made but refused, the unsuccessful party cannot make another without the consent of the court or the agreement of the other party.

Breach not proved – costs consequences

66. If the court does not find the breach is proved, the committal application must be dismissed, and the applicant may be

---

[190] Section 12 and Schedule 2

required to pay the defendant's costs, depending on the circumstances of the dismissal.

67. There is a significant advantage to a legally aided defendant in obtaining a costs order against the applicant authority. The hourly rate paid by the LAB is very low, whereas if a costs order is made against the applicant, they can claim the full hourly Guideline Rates for the area, currently in the region of £260 an hour for a solicitor. This would make an unsuccessful committal application very expensive to the applicant.

68. Even if the committal application is dismissed there may be reasons why no order for costs may be the appropriate outcome. The court will be slow to penalising costs and applicant who is pursuing a public function, particularly where it involves the protection of the public. Additionally, a defendant may be fortunate to be able to rely on a technical defence, or they have brought the committal proceedings onto themselves.

CHAPTER FIFTEEN
VARIATION AND DISCHARGE

KEY POINTS

1. The 2014 Act expressly allows the Court to vary or discharge injunctions
2. Procedure
3. Exclusion orders on variations
4. Applications to discharge
5. Hearings of applications to vary or discharge
6. Consequences of dismissal of an application

Introduction

1. Prior to the making of a final order, at a subsequent or final hearing the court may vary the interim order.

2. If there has been a breach of the final order or the facts have changed, eg nuisance may have continued or the injunction may be about to expire, or behaviour may change in nature, becoming more or less of a problem. Once an interim order has been converted into a final injunction, it may therefore be necessary to apply to change it.

3. The Court is still entitled under the 2014 Act[191] to vary a final order on the application of either party, or of its own motion under CPR 3.3. While this can sometimes be done without formal application at a committal hearing (either by agreement or by order of the judge), it is otherwise necessary to file an N244 with supporting evidence.

4. If a perpetrator continues to cause a nuisance and the original term of the injunction is about to expire, an application must be commenced well before it is due to run out (e.g. a couple of months if possible), because otherwise the court may struggle to list a hearing before the expiry of the order.

5. It is much more expensive to make a fresh application for an injunction than to apply to continue an existing one. This also avoids the evidential difficulties caused by having two separate claims in existence in relation to the same property/defendant.

Procedure

6. An application must be made pursuant to CPR 23. Rules of Court distinguish between applications to vary or discharge an injunction under s 42 of the 2009 Act, which can be made without notice, and injunctions made under the 2014 Act, which by implication have to be made on notice.

7. The application has to be made with supporting evidence and it will help to focus the witness statements on:

    - the defendant's response to the making of the order and the history of compliance;

[191] under the power given to it in section 8 of the Act, and complying with CPR 65.45 and CPR 23

- the effect of any continuing ASB on victims;
- the events leading to the decision to request variation;
- the justification for each new term;
- ancillary matters such as extension of the duration, amendments to the power of arrest etc.

Expiry of the original injunction pending hearing

8. Given the significant delays between receipt of applications by the court office and the date listed for hearing, an application for the extension of an injunction may well be listed after it has already expired.

9. It may be necessary to ask in the N244 for an interim extension of the order of the court's own motion under CPR 3.3. It is important to repeat that request in the letter or email accompanying the application and to stress its urgency. If the application is adjourned, it is necessary to ensure that the wording of the ex-parte or interim application extension covers the period before the final hearing and is not limited simply to a date.

10. Applications to vary can include the addition of new prohibitions or positive requirements, or the variation or removal of an existing one, the extension or reduction of the length of validity of the order or the addition or removal of a power of arrest.192

Exclusion orders on variation

11. The ability to vary an injunction can provide it with substantially more teeth than it possessed upon grant. If nuisance continues and worsens, it may become necessary to vary an order to include

[192] see the guidance at paragraph 125

an exclusion, either from an area, or from the defendant's own home.

12. This power may be particularly useful in more serious cases, either as a means of evicting a non-tenant partner, or as a precursor to eviction of the tenant, although of course it cannot be used against an under 18-year-old.

Applications to discharge

13. In rare cases, an applicant or defendant may apply to discharge an injunction, although more commonly they simply expire.

14. Applications to discharge may be made by either side. They can be particularly important if a defendant is a tenant who wishes to engage in a mutual exchange of their tenancy. Many housing providers prohibit mutual exchanges if an injunction is in force against a tenant.

Hearing of application to vary

15. The format of any hearing will depend on the nature of the allegations and the variation sought. In some circumstances it may be possible to persuade the court to make the order without a hearing, relying on CPR 3.3. The court should be reminded of the need to insert in the order a statement of the right to make an application to set the order aside, or to vary or stay it under CPR 3.3 (5).

16. When such an application is made, a draft of the suggested amended injunction order should be included with the application, together with a draft of the General Form of Order which the court will need to make if it agrees to vary the order.

17. In other cases, the defendant may object to the variation sought and ask the court to hear evidence on the necessity for the

variation. This is equally true on any application by a defendant to vary or discharge the order.

Consequences of dismissal of an application

18. If an application to vary or discharge an injunction is dismissed, that applicant cannot make another application without permission of the court or the consent of the other party.[193] In practice this provision is rarely used.

[193] Section 8(4)

CHAPTER SIXTEEN
OTHER REMEDIES

KEY POINTS

1. Criminal behaviour orders
2. Dispersal powers
3. Community Protection Notices
4. Public Spaces Protection Orders
5. Closure orders
6. Mandatory and discretionary grounds of possession

1. The other remedies created by the 2014 Act reflect an amalgamation and development of previously available powers.

Criminal Behaviour Orders

2. Criminal behaviour orders are imposed on conviction in the criminal courts and they replace ASBOs. They are intended for use against only a small percentage of the criminal population who "*represent the most persistently antisocial individuals who are also engaged in criminal activity*".

3. The standard of proof is set at the criminal level, requiring the prosecution to prove beyond reasonable doubt that the defendant has behaved in a manner which is likely to cause harassment, alarm or distress.

4. The maximum penalty for breach of an adult CBO is five years imprisonment and/or an unlimited fine.

Dispersal powers

5. These powers are only available to the police and community support officers. They provide short-term relief to the general public, requiring those given the direction to leave an area for up to 48-hours.

6. They can be used in respect of behaviour which contributes, or is likely to contribute to members of the public being harassed, alarmed or distressed and the order is necessary to reduce or remove the likelihood of ASB, crime or disorder.

7. Breach of a Dispersal Direction is a criminal offence, punishable by a Level 4 fine or up to 3 months in prison for over 18-year-olds.

Community Protection Notices

8. Such notices are intended for use in cases of minor ASB and nuisance which "spoils the community's quality-of-life".

9. They are particularly useful as an addition to the powers under s 79 of the Environmental Protection Act 1990. They were intended to replace the number of existing remedies, addressing problems like litter control.

10. Breach of a CPN is punishable by a fixed penalty notice of up to £100 or a level 4 fine for individuals, or £20,000 for businesses.

Public Spaces Protection Orders

11. PSPOs are intended to prevent ASB in public places by individuals or groups. They can be issued by local authorities

after consultation with the police, the Police and Crime Commissioner and other bodies.

12. They are relevant when the behaviour is having or is likely to have a detrimental effect on the quality of life of people in the area, is persistent and unreasonable.

13. Breach is a criminal offence and punishable with a fixed penalty notice of up to £100 or a fine on the level 3 if prosecuted.

14. While they should not be used to control homeless people or rough sleepers, they can be employed eg, to control dog walkers in appropriate circumstances.

Closure orders

15. The power to order the closure of premises is designed to assist in cases of serious ASB associated with a particular building or land. They are particularly useful in cases where a property is being used for serious drug-dealing or the like.

16. They allow the police or a local authority to apply for an order if there is likely to be a public nuisance or disorder in or around premises.

17. A Closure Notice can be imposed for up to 48-hours in respect of situations where nuisance to the public or disorder near premises has occurred or will occur if the order is not made.

18. In more serious cases a Closure Order can be obtained from a Magistrates' Court, lasting for up to 6 months where there is disorderly, offensive or criminal behaviour, serious nuisance to the public or disorder near premises.

19. Breach of a Notice is punishable by up to 3 months' imprisonment and breach of an Order carries a six-month maximum sentence. Both can give result in an unlimited fine.

Mandatory and discretionary grounds of possession

20. Finally, the 2014 Act introduced Ground 7A an absolute ground for possession of social and private housing tenancies where another court has found proved allegations of antisocial behaviour or certain types of criminality.

21. They can be used when a tenant or a member of their household has been convicted of certain crimes specified in Schedule 2A of the Housing Act 1985, or where they have breached an ASBI, a CBO, or a noise abatement notice. They will also be available where a property has been closed for more than 48-hours under a Closure Order.

22. Secure tenants have a statutory right to ask for a review of the decision and other social landlords are encouraged to adopt such a procedure. Invariably they do so as it would otherwise lead to a challenge to the procedural fairness of the measure.

23. If the offence or breach is of the listed type, and occurred in the locality of the property or it affected someone with a right to live in the locality, or the landlord or their staff etc, then the court must grant a possession order.

24. However human rights defences are available, including the right to challenge the proportionality of the action and to ensure that the correct procedure has been followed.

25. Any detailed discussion of the application of the mandatory ground is beyond the scope of this book and is addressed in textbooks on possession claims.

PRECEDENTS

1. N16A Application Notice for Interim Injunction
2. N16 Injunction Order
3. N110A Draft Power of Arrest
4. Witness Statement in support
5. N600 Contempt Application
6. N601 Summons on Contempt Application
7. N602 Arrest Warrant
8. N603 Order on Contempt Application
9. N604 Warrant of Committal

N16A Application Notice for Interim Injunction

Application for Injunction (General Form)

Name of court	Claim No.
Claimant's Name and Ref.	
Defendant's Name and Ref.	
Fee Account no.	

Notes on completion

Tick which boxes apply and specify the legislation where appropriate

(1) Enter the full name of the person making the application

(2) Enter the full name of the person the injunction is to be directed to

(3) Set out any proposed orders requiring acts to be done. Delete if no mandatory order is sought.

(4) Set out here the proposed terms of the injunction order (if the defendant is a limited company delete the wording in brackets and insert 'whether by its servants, agents, officers or otherwise').

(5) Set out here any further terms asked for including provision for costs

(6) Enter the names of all persons who have sworn affidavits or signed statements in support of this application

(7) Enter the names and addresses of all persons upon whom it is intended to serve this application

(8) Enter the full name and address for service and delete as required

☐ By application in pending proceedings

☐ Under Statutory provision ____________________

☐ This application is made under Part 8 of the Civil Procedure Rules

Seal

This application raises issues under the Human Rights Act 1998 ☐ Yes ☐ No

The Claimant[(1)]

applies to the court for an injunction order in the following terms:

The Defendant[(2)]

must[(3)]

The Defendant

be forbidden (whether by himself or by instructing or encouraging or permitting any other person)[(4)]

And that[(5)]

The grounds of this application are set out in the written evidence

of[(6)] sworn (signed) on

This written evidence is served with this application.

This application is to be served upon[(7)]

This application is filed by[(8)]

(the Solicitors for) the Claimant (Applicant/Petitioner)

whose address for service is

Signed Dated

This section to be completed by the court

* Name and address of the person application is directed to

To*

of

This application will be heard by the (District) Judge

at

on **the** **day of** **20** **at** **o'clock**

If you do not attend at the time shown the court may make an injunction order in your absence

If you do not fully understand this application you should go to a Solicitor, Legal Advice Centre or a Citizens' Advice Bureau

The court office at

is open between 10am and 4pm Mon - Fri. When corresponding with the court, please address all forms and letters to the Court Manager and quote the claim number.

N16A General form of application for injunction (05.14)

N16 Injunction Order

Click here to reset form | Click here to print form

Injunction order

Name of court	
Claim no.	
Claimant's ref.	
Defendant's ref.	
For completion by the court Issued on	

Claimant's name

Defendant's name

Seal

If you do not comply with this order you may be held in contempt of court and imprisoned or fined, or your assets may be seized.

Enter date

On the the court considered an application for an injuction.

Enter the name of the person the order is directed to below

The court ordered that

Has a mandatory order been made? ☐ Yes ☐ No

Enter below the time and place as ordered

on or before

If you do not understand anything in this order you should go to a solicitor, Legal Advice Centre or a Citizens Advice Bureau

The court office at

is open between 10 am and 4 pm Monday to Friday. When corresponding with the court, please address forms or letters to the Court Manager and quote the claim number.

N16 General form of injunction for interim application or originating application (10.12)

Is the defendant a Limited Company? ☐ Yes ☐ No

and is forbidden whether by himself or by instructing or encouraging or permitting any other person from

Enter date Enter time

This order will remain in force until the at

unless before then it is revoked by a further order of the court.

Enter the terms of any orders, costs etc.

It is further ordered that

The applicant do pay the costs of the application

If the power of arrest is not applicable tick box

A power of arrest be attached to clauses

Is the order temporary and made without notice? ☐ Yes ☐ No

Notice of further hearing

The court will reconsider the application and whether the order should continue at a further hearing at:

Enter name of court

Enter date Enter time

on the at

If you do not attend at the time shown the court may make an injunction order in your absence.

You are entitled to apply to the court to re-consider the order before that day.

If you do not understand anything in this order you should go to a solicitor, Legal Advice Centre or a Citizens Advice Bureau

Injunction order - Record of hearing

Claim no.

Enter date
On

Enter name of judge
Before District Judge

Enter court address
The court was sitting at

The claimant

was ☐ represented by Counsel

☐ represented by a Solicitor

☐ in person

The defendant

was ☐ represented by Counsel

☐ represented by a Solicitor

☐ in person

☐ did not appear having been given notice of this hearing

☐ not given notice of this hearing

The court read the written evidence of

☐ the claimant sworn on (Enter date)

☐ the defendant sworn on (Enter date)

And of signed on (Enter date)

sworn on (Enter date)

The court heard spoken evidence on oath from

Delete this paragraph if the court does not require the undertaking ☐ Delete

The claimant gave an undertaking (through his counsel or solicitor) promising to pay any damages ordered by the court if it later decides that the defendant has suffered loss or damage as a result of this order.

Signed (Judges clerk) Dated

Click here to reset form | Click here to print form

N110A Draft Power of Arrest

N110A

Power of arrest

Name of court	**Claim No.**
Claimant's name (including ref.)	
Defendant's name (including ref.)	

Name of defendant

Defendant's address

Seal

Date order made ☐☐/☐☐/☐☐☐☐ Name of judge

Order made under (insert statutory provision)

This order includes a power of arrest under (insert statutory provision)

The relevant paragraphs of the order to which a power of arrest has been attached are:
(set out those paragraphs of the order to which the power of arrest is attached, if necessary continue on a separate sheet)

This power of arrest was ordered on ☐☐/☐☐/☐☐☐☐ **and expires on the** ☐☐/☐☐/☐☐☐☐

Note to Arresting Officer

Where the defendant is arrested under the power given by section 155 of the Housing Act 1996, or section 27 of the Police and Justice Act 2006; or section 43 of the Policing and Crime Act 2009; or section 4 of the Anti-Social Behaviour, Crime and Policing Act 2014:-

- the defendant shall be brought before the judge within the period of 24 hours beginning at the time of their arrest;
- a constable shall inform the person on whose application the injunction was granted, forthwith where the defendant is arrested under the power given by section 155 of the Housing Act 1996 or as soon as reasonably practicable where the defendant is arrested under the power given by section 27 of the Police and Justice Act 2006 or section 43 of the Policing and Crime Act 2009 or section 4 of the Anti-Social Behaviour, Crime and Policing Act 2014.

Nothing in section 155 of the Housing Act 1996 or section 27 of the Police and Justice Act 2006 or section 43 of the Policing and Crime Act 2009 or section 4 of the Anti-Social Behaviour, Crime and Policing Act 2014, shall authorise the detention of the respondent after the expiry of the period of 24 hours beginning at the time of their arrest.

In calculating any period of 24 hours, no account shall be taken of Christmas Day, Good Friday or any Sunday.

Name of Claimant

Claimant's address

Claimant's phone number

Print form Reset form

N110A Power of arrest attached to injunction (06.15)

Witness Statement in support

i) Statement of Sarah Siddons
ii) Statement: First
iii) For: Claimant
iv) Dated: 25/04/23
v) Exhibits: SS/1-/7

IN THE COUNTY COURT AT ANY TOWN

CLAIM NO: D00SE545

B E T W E E N:

ANY HOUSING ASSOCIATION LIMITED

Claimant

and

(1) MS SARAH SMITH

First Defendant

(2) MR JOHN PERCIVAL

Second Defendant

WITNESS STATEMENT OF SARAH SIDDONS

I SARAH SIDDONS, OF ANY HOUSING ASSOCIATION, A BUSINESS PARK, ANY TOWN, LB2 6GH, WILL SAY AS FOLLOWS:-

1 I am employed by the Claimant as an Antisocial Behaviour Officer. I make this statement from matters which are within my own knowledge and belief, save where otherwise indicated. I have been involved in this case since June 2021 when I carried out a joint visit with the First Defendant's Housing Officer, Erica Jenkins.

2 I make this statement in support of injunction proceedings against the two defendants named above.

3 This application is being made on an urgent basis, given the events that occurred on Monday and yesterday. As is evident from the contents of this witness statement and exhibits and that of the named witness, there is a significant risk of harm, both physical and mental to other residents in the locality of the property concerned and to visitors to the area.

4 For that reason, it has not been possible to go through the steps in the Pre-Action Protocol for ASBIs, although consideration has already been given prior to the decision to apply for a possession order to the First Defendant's personal circumstances and mental health/vulnerabilities.

5 Further, there is a real urgency in pursuing this application, particularly given the nature of the violence perpetrated by the Second Defendant against the resident who has provided a witness statement, together with the threats and intimidation by the First Defendant. The Claimant is seeking a power of arrest on all the provisions of the injunction against each Defendant, for reasons which should be evident upon reading this witness statement.

6 Although this application is not being brought 'on notice', because I am asking for the Second Defendant to be excluded from the property, I intend to inform the Defendants that I am making the application and to serve them tomorrow morning, in time for them to attend the hearing in the afternoon if they wish to do so.

7 I have ascertained from both the victims of the intimidation and violence that they will be out at work by 8 AM tomorrow morning. Assuming the injunction is granted, I intend to serve on the defendants a copy of the injunction and power of arrest before the victims return from work. As a result, I confident that there will be no real opportunity for any further witness intimidation before the hearing.

8 The First Defendant is Ms Sarah Smith (dob 15.04.03, now 20 years old) who has an assured tenancy at Flat 24 Any Road, Any Town, LB13 4QT ("the Property"). A copy of this is shown to me, marked "**Exhibit SS/1**". There are various provisions in the tenancy, at clause …., relating to nuisance and antisocial behaviour.

9 The Second Defendant is the First Defendant's partner, Mr John Percival (dob 2.1.98, now 25 years old).

10 The property is a two-bedroom ground floor flat which is situated in a small development of 10 properties, which are owned and managed by the Claimant. An HMLR Office Copy Entry and plan of the area, together with photos of the block and the rear of the property are shown to me and produced, marked "**Exhibit SS/2**".

11 The First Defendant has held this tenancy since 22/06/22, for just over 10 months.

12 Just after the tenancy began, the Second Defendant moved into the property. He is well known to the local police and to the Claimant as being a perpetrator of nuisance and domestic violence at another

property owned by the Claimant; he is addicted to crack cocaine and has been convicted of possession with intent to supply a 'Class A' substance (heroin) and of burglary of dwelling houses. He was in prison until early 2022 when he was released having served just under three years of a five-year sentence. Had we known that he was planning to move into the property, we would not have granted the tenancy.

13 Reports of anti-social behaviour from the property and of nuisance to neighbours began immediately and residents in the locality began to contact the Claimant about this behaviour and the effect on the First Defendant's children.

14 The Claimant also reported these concerns and the behaviour to Social Services, who investigated them and quickly placed all three into care with foster parents.

15 The chronology of incidents can be summarised as follows:

15.1 25/6/22….

16 I have prepared a "Scott Schedule" which sets out these incidents in chronological order. It identifies the witness statement and paragraph number pertinent to the particular allegation. A copy will be provided to the Court separately to this statement.

17 The Claimant initially responded by giving the First Defendant a number of verbal and written warnings about the antisocial behaviour and by asking her to require the Second Defendant to leave. The letters which I wrote to the First Defendant are shown to me and produced, marked "**Exhibit SS3**". I telephoned her on the following occasions:

17.1 12.7.22…

18 Then, on 5.10.22 I visited the Property. The First Defendant was home to meet me as arranged, but she was so abusive on the doorstep that I terminated the interview without entering.

19 Subsequent to this contact, the First Defendant's conduct did not improve and even after being told in writing that her tenancy was at risk, she refused to ask the Second Defendant to move out. Subsequently, given the continuing antisocial behaviour, I met with my manager and we decided to end the tenancy because of serious anti-social behaviour.

20 An assessment was carried out to consider the proportionality of our intended action. No vulnerabilities were disclosed by the tenant in her housing application and none are known to the Claimant at this date. A referral to drug and alcohol treatment was attempted, but the tenant rejected any suggestion that she needed help, and threatened the staff member who suggested it. She also said that she didn't care that her and her partner's behaviour were putting her tenancy at risk as she hated her neighbours and didn't want to stay in the property. There is now produced and shown to me, **marked SS/4**, a copy of the assessment and of the internal records of the attempt at referral.

21 On 3.12.22 I served her personally with a Section 8 notice seeking possession. This notice has expired and possession proceedings have been issued. Regrettably the court has not been able to provide a date for the first hearing. A copy of the notice, accompanying letter and certificate of service are shown to me and produced marked "**Exhibit SS/5**".

22 When the notice was served, despite what she said earlier about not wanting the property, the First Defendant said she would go to solicitors and defend the claim, although I have not received any notification that she has instructed lawyers on her behalf.

23 Initially, for the period over Christmas after service of the notice, the nuisance greatly reduced, but I have subsequently discovered this was only because the Second Defendant had been remanded in custody on other charges. He was released on bail and the nuisance and other antisocial behaviour recommenced immediately.

24 I have received complaints from three sets of neighbours, although two households are so scared of the Second Defendant that they have refused to come to court to give evidence or even to be named as witnesses. However, they have agreed to provide anonymised witness statements, with the nuisance logs attached to them.

25 There is now shown to me and produced, marked "**Exhibit SS/6**", a copy of the two witness statements provided by the members of those households. I confirm that they are both within 50 m of the First Defendant's flat. This witness statements contain evidence of the incidents which had occurred up to 15.4.23 and were due to be used in the possession proceedings.

26 Regrettably, a serious incident occurred on Monday, in which the First Defendant threatened and intimidated one of the witnesses, a Miss Barbara Powell, who has given a witness statement and is prepared to attend court. I refer to the content of that statement for a description of the events of that afternoon. They resulted in the arrest of the First Defendant.

27 Then, yesterday, at around 3 PM, the Second Defendant went around to Miss Powell's flat, knocked on the door. When it was opened by Miss Powell's partner, the Second Defendant headbutted him without any provocation. It has not been possible to take a witness statement from him yet as he was knocked unconscious and has not yet been released from hospital, but I refer to the content of Miss Powell's witness statement. She was present at the time,

standing directly behind her partner and witnessed the whole incident. Again, police were called and the Second Defendant was arrested, although due to an oversight at the police station, he was released on police bail and has returned to the property.

28 As a result of those incidents, my manager and I decided that an urgent application was necessary to exclude the Second Defendant from the property as soon as possible. This application is being pursued with a view to his being required to leave as soon as possible and in any event within four days.

29 I obtained a Community Impact Statement from PC Frost at Any County Police for use in the possession proceedings. He has described the significant problems caused by both defendants, and the fear and distress which they and their associates are creating. A copy of this is shown to me and produced, marked "**Exhibit SS/7**".

30 Some of the evidence on which I rely is hearsay. I have read the Civil Evidence Act 1995 and have used it to consider whether the anonymous hearsay evidence which I am producing for the Court might be inaccurate. Section 4 (2) the Act says:

"Regard may be had, in particular, to the following –

(a) whether it would have been reasonable and practicable for the party by whom the evidence was adduced to have produced the maker of the original statement as a witness;

(b) whether the original statement was made contemporaneously with the occurrence or existence of the matters stated;

(c) whether the evidence involves multiple hearsay;

(d) whether any person involved had any motive to conceal or misrepresent matters;

(e) whether the original statement was an edited account, or was made in collaboration with another or for a particular purpose;

(f) whether the circumstances in which the evidence is adducted as hearsay are such as to suggest an attempt to prevent proper evaluation of its weight."

31 Having spoken to these residents myself, I believe they are telling the truth and are reliable and trustworthy. They have told me that the Second Defendant has often been heard in the street boasting about the violence he uses against others and saying that no one will ever give evidence against him. I confirm that I do not believe that there has been concealment or misrepresentation; and that they only want to remain anonymous due to their fears that some harm may be caused to them at the hands of the Defendants or their visitors.

32 It is not practicable for the Claimant to produce the makers of the statements as a result of their fear. The evidence is not edited and there has been no attempt to prevent proper evaluation of its weight- I have tried to record their words as accurately as possible.

33 I ask the Court to grant an injunction which stops these Defendants from engaging in antisocial behaviour and also excludes the Second Defendant from the property with effect from 4 PM next Monday. Given the difficulties he has caused other properties owned by the Claimant, I would also ask that the injunction extends to exclude him from any property owned by the Claimant once he is aware of its ownership, and prevents him from attending any of the Claimant's office premises.

STATEMENT OF TRUTH

I believe that the facts stated in this witness statement are true I understand that proceedings for contempt of court may be brought against anyone who makes, or causes to be made, a false statement in a document verified by a statement of truth without an honest belief in its truth.

Signed..

Dated...

N600 Contempt Application

Contempt application

(other than an application under Part 8) CPR 81.3 and 81.4

Name of court

Claim no.

Claimant's name (including ref.)

Defendant's name (including ref.)

Date

Day	Month	Year

1. What is your name or, if you are a legal representative, the name of your firm?

2. Are you a

☐ Claimant

☐ Legal representative of the claimant

3. Who should be served with this application?

First name(s)

Last name

4. Please give the service address of any party named in question 3

Building and street

Second line of address

Town or city

County (optional)

Postcode

The written evidence of the claimant in support of this application, in the form of an affidavit or affirmation, is attached to this application

If permission is required to make this application, the application for permission (headed 'Application for permission') must be included in this application

To the defendant

If upon determination of this application you are held to be in contempt of court you may be imprisoned or fined, or your assets may be seized

Your rights

You have the right to be legally represented in the contempt proceedings.

You are entitled to a reasonable opportunity to obtain legal representation and to apply for legal aid which may be available without any means test.

You may be entitled to the services of an interpreter.

You are entitled to a reasonable time to prepare for the hearing of the contempt application against you.

You are entitled but not obliged to give written and oral evidence in your defence.

You have the right to remain silent and may not be compelled to answer any question the answer to which may incriminate you.

If you do not attend the hearing, the court may proceed in your absence. Whether or not you attend, the court will only find you in contempt if satisfied beyond reasonable doubt of the facts constituting contempt and that they do constitute contempt.

If the court is satisfied that you have committed a contempt, the court may punish you by a fine, imprisonment, confiscation of assets or other punishment permitted under the law.

If you admit the contempt and wish to apologise to the court, that is likely to reduce the seriousness of any punishment by the court.

The court's findings will be provided in writing as soon as practicable after the hearing.

The court will sit in public, unless and to the extent that the court orders otherwise. Its findings will be made public.

The following information is required to be included in the application pursuant to rule 81.4(2) of the Civil Procedure Rules 1998.

5. Nature of the contempt (for example, breach of an order or undertaking or contempt in the face of the court)

6. Is the application based on breach of an order?

☐ Yes – **go to question 7**

☐ No – **go to question 10**

7. Date and terms of the order allegedly breached or disobeyed ('the order'). (If there is more than one such order, set out the date and terms of each order.)

8. Date of personal service of the order

Day	Month	Year

If the order was not personally served, state the date and terms of any order dispensing with personal service of the order.

9. Did the order include a penal notice?

☐ Yes

☐ No

10. Date and the terms of any undertaking allegedly breached ('the undertaking'). (If there is more than one such undertaking set out the date and terms of each undertaking.)

11. Does the claimant, believe that the person who gave the undertaking understood its terms and the consequences of failure to comply with it?

☐ Yes

☐ No

12. Summary of facts alleged to constitute the contempt (set these out very briefly, in chronological order, in numbered points)

Statement of Truth

I understand that proceedings for contempt of court may be brought against anyone who makes, or causes to be made, a false statement in a document verified by a statement of truth without an honest belief in its truth.

☐ **I believe** that the facts stated in this contempt application are true.

☐ **The Claimant believes** that the facts stated in this contempt application are true.

Signature for the Statement of Truth

☐ Claimant

☐ Litigation friend

☐ Claimant's legal representative

Date

Day Month Year

Full name

Name of Claimant's legal representative's firm

Position or office held (if signing on behalf of a company)

Signature for the Contempt application

☐ Claimant

☐ Litigation friend

☐ Claimant's legal representative

Date

Day Month Year

Full name

Name of Claimant's legal representative's firm

Position or office held (if signing on behalf of a company)

Claimant's address to which documents about this application should be sent

Building and street

Second line of address

Town or city

County (optional)

Postcode

Page 8

Phone number

Email address

Fax number

DX number

Reference number

Page 9

Court fee

What you need to pay

The court fee for this application is **£275**

How to pay the court fee

- ☐ I attached a **Cheque/Postal order,** made payable to 'HMCTS'
- ☐ **A debit/credit card payment**
  - ☐ I will pay over the phone, please call me on the number below
  - ☐ please email me details on how to pay, my email address is
- ☐ **Prepayment –** If you have already made a payment please note the reference number here

  Your reference

- ☐ **In person at** the court/office
- ☐ **I have not included payment because**
  - ☐ I have applied for Help with Fees online and my reference number is

H	W	F						

  - ☐ I am applying for Help with Fees, see attached form **EX160**
  - ☐ Other – please explain why
- ☐ **Payment by account –** for use by legal professionals

  Your account number

P	B	A							

  Your reference (if applicable)

What if I cannot afford to pay a court fee?

You may not have to pay a fee, or you may get some money off it if you only have a small amount of savings and investments, receive certain benefits or are on a low income. This is sometimes known as 'fee remission.'

You can apply for help with court and tribunal fees online at www.gov.uk/help-with-court-fees or through the 'EX160 Apply for help with fees' form and 'EX160A – How to apply for help with fees' guidance.

N601 Summons on Contempt Application

Summons to appear at court for directions to be given

(issued under rule 81.6(1) and (3) of the Civil Procedure Rules 1998)

This is an important legal document requiring you to attend court. You should read it carefully and you are advised to obtain independent legal advice.

If upon determination of the matters raised in this summons you are held to be in contempt of court you may be imprisoned or fined, or your assets may be seized.

Claim no.

Claimant's name (including ref.)

Defendant's name (including ref.)

To the defendant

Name

Building and street

Second line of address

Town or city

County (optional)

Postcode

Note – Give the address of defendant at which summons to be served

You are summoned to appear at the court listed below for directions to be given.

Name of court

Building and street

Second line of address

Town or city

County (optional)

Postcode

Time of hearing

Date of hearing

Day Month Year

If you do not attend the court on the date and at the time stated above a warrant may be issued for your arrest and production at the court.

This summons has been issued by the above court because it appears to

Name and rank of judge

that you may have committed a contempt of court.

Note – This summons has been issued under rule 81.6(1) and (3) of the Civil Procedure Rules 1998

To the defendant

Your rights

You have the right to be legally represented in the contempt proceedings.

You are entitled to a reasonable opportunity to obtain legal representation and to apply for legal aid which may be available without any means test.

You may be entitled to the services of an interpreter.

You are entitled to a reasonable time to prepare for the hearing of the contempt application against you.

You are entitled but not obliged to give written and oral evidence in your defence.

You have the right to remain silent and may not be compelled to answer any question the answer to which may incriminate you.

If you do not attend the hearing, the court may proceed in your absence. Whether or not you attend, the court will only find you in contempt if satisfied beyond reasonable doubt of the facts constituting contempt and that they do constitute contempt.

If the court is satisfied that you have committed a contempt, the court may punish you by a fine, imprisonment, confiscation of assets or other punishment permitted under the law.

If you admit the contempt and wish to apologise to the court, that is likely to reduce the seriousness of any punishment by the court.

The court's findings will be provided in writing as soon as practicable after the hearing.

The court will sit in public, unless and to the extent that the court orders otherwise. Its findings will be made public.

The following information is required to be included in the summons pursuant to rule 81.6(3) of the Civil Procedure Rules 1998.

4. Nature of the contempt (for example, breach of an order or undertaking or contempt in the face of the court)

5. Is the summons based on the breach of an order?

- ☐ Yes – **go to question 6**
- ☐ No – **go to question 9**

6. Date and terms of the order allegedly breached or disobeyed ('the order'). (If there is more than one such order, set out the date and terms of each order.)

7. Date of personal service of the order

Day Month Year

If the order was not personally served state the date and terms of any order dispensing with personal service of the order

8. Did the order include a penal notice warning of the potential consequences of failure to comply?

☐ Yes

☐ No

9. Date and the terms of any undertaking allegedly breached ('the undertaking'). (If there is more than one such undertaking, set out the date and terms of each undertaking)

10. Did the person who gave the undertaking understand its terms and the consequences of failure to comply with it?

☐ Yes

☐ No

11. Summary of facts alleged to constitute the contempt (set these out very briefly, in chronological order, in numbered points)

When you appear at court, directions will be given by the judge for determining the allegation(s) of contempt of court against you or a substantive order may be made on this summons if appropriate.

Signature

☐ Judge of the High Court

☐ Judge of the County Court

Dated

Day Month Year

N602 Arrest Warrant

Warrant to secure attendance at court

(issued under rule 81.7(2) of the Civil Procedure Rules)

To:

☐ the Tipstaff (if in the High Court), attending on His Majesty's High Court of Justice, their deputy or assistants, and

☐ all police constables whom it may concern

Claim no.

Claimant's name (including ref.)

Defendant's name (including ref.)

☐ **A contempt application** having been made in this claim for an order determining proceedings for contempt of court;

and an order having been made on

Day Month Year

for the defendant to attend for a directions hearing or a substantive hearing.

Defendant's name

Note – Contempt application made under rules 81.3 and 81.4 of the Civil Procedure Rules.

OR

☐ **A summons** having been issued in this claim for the attendance of the defendant to answer an allegation of contempt of court.

Defendant's name

Note – A summons issued under rule 81.6 of the Civil Procedure Rules.

And the defendant having failed personally to appear before the judge as required.*

*delete the words 'as required' if appropriate

N602 Warrant to secure attendance at court (10.22)

Page 1

This warrant commands you and every one of you to apprehend the defendant

and bring them before a judge of this court at

Time

Date

Day Month Year

or as soon as possible thereafter to be dealt with according to law.

If you apprehend the defendant after 4.00pm they shall be held in custody until such time as the Court shall next sit.

Signature

☐ Judge of the High Court

☐ Judge of the County Court

Dated

Day Month Year

N603 Order on Contempt Application

Order on determination of proceedings for contempt of court

(issued under rule 81.9(1) of the Civil Procedure Rules)

Name of court

Claim no.

Claimant's name (including ref.)

Defendant's name (including ref.)

After hearing counsel for the claimant and for the defendant

And after

☐ considering an application by the claimant for an order determining contempt proceedings

☐ considering a summons issued rule under 81.6(3) of the Civil Procedure Rules

☐ reading the evidence filed by the parties and hearing oral evidence at the hearing of the application or summons

Note – In this order, 'claimant' means the person making the contempt application and 'defendant' means the person against whom the application was made.

The court being satisfied beyond reasonable doubt that the defendant is guilty of contempt of court

☐ in the manner stated in the court's judgment

☐ by breaching an order of the court made on

Day	Month	Year

N603 Order on determination of proceedings for contempt of court (08.21)

Page 1

☐ by breaching an undertaking given to the court on

Day	Month	Year

not to (state breach of undertaking etc.)

AND the matters required by Civil Procedure Rule 81.4(2) having been included in the

☐ application

☐ summons

It is ordered that:

1. ☐ The defendant be committed to prison for a period of

Days	Weeks	Months	Years

2. ☐ The committal of the defendant to prison under paragraph 1 above shall be suspended on the following terms - set out terms below

3. ☐ The defendant shall pay to HM Courts & Tribunals Service a fine of

£ ____ **within** ____ **days**

4. ☐ The relevant commissioners authorised for the purpose by the claimant and to be approved by the court shall be authorised at the request of the claimant to confiscate, seize and sequester the following real and personal property of the defendant

until they clear

☐ their contempt **or**

☐ until further order

5. ☐ The defendant shall pay the claimant's costs

☐ on the indemnity basis

☐ summarily assessed in the sum of

£ ☐

☐ to be subject to detailed assessment, if not agreed.

6. The defendant may apply under rule 81.10 of the Civil Procedure Rules 1998 to discharge this order.

7. The defendant has the right to appeal.

8. The court before which any appeal must be brought is

9. The Appellant's Notice must be filed at the appeal court by 4pm on

Day	Month	Year

10. A transcript of the judgment given at this hearing will be published on the website of the judiciary of England and Wales.

Dated

Day	Month	Year

N604 Warrant of Committal

Warrant of committal

(issued under rule 81.9(2) of the Civil Procedure Rules 1998)

To:

☐ the Tipstaff (if in the High Court), attending on His Majesty's High Court of Justice, their deputy or assistants, and

☐ the officers of the court and all police constables whom it may concern

Name of court

Claim no.

Claimant's name (including ref.)

Defendant's name (including ref.)

By the order of committal of this court given this day it was ordered that the defendant

stands committed to HM Prison for their contempt as set out in the order.

This warrant commands you and every one of you in His Majesty's name to apprehend the defendant and convey them safely to HM Prison at

to be detained there and kept in safe custody for a period of

from the date of their apprehension or until further order.

Signature

Dated

Day Month Year

Judge of the

☐ High Court

☐ County Court

N604 Warrant of committal (10.22)

Page 1

INDEX

'A Practical Guide to Hoarding and Mental Health for Housing Lawyers' by Rachel Coyle
'A Practical Guide to Psychiatric Claims in Personal Injury – 2nd Edition' by Liam Ryan
'Stephens on Contractual Indemnities' by Richard Stephens
'A Practical Guide to the EU Succession Regulation' by Richard Frimston
'A Practical Guide to Solicitor and Client Costs – 2nd Edition' by Robin Dunne
'Constructive Dismissal – Practice Pointers and Principles' by Benjimin Burgher
'A Practical Guide to Religion and Belief Discrimination Claims in the Workplace' by Kashif Ali
'A Practical Guide to the Law of Medical Treatment Decisions' by Ben Troke
'Fundamental Dishonesty and QOCS in Personal Injury Proceedings: Law and Practice' by Jake Rowley
'A Practical Guide to the Law in Relation to School Exclusions' by Charlotte Hadfield & Alice de Coverley
'A Practical Guide to Divorce for the Silver Separators' by Karin Walker
'The Right to be Forgotten – The Law and Practical Issues' by Melissa Stock
'A Practical Guide to Planning Law and Rights of Way in National Parks, the Broads and AONBs' by James Maurici QC, James Neill et al
'A Practical Guide to Election Law' by Tom Tabori
'A Practical Guide to the Law in Relation to Surrogacy' by Andrew Powell
'A Practical Guide to Claims Arising from Fatal Accidents – 2nd Edition' by James Patience
'A Practical Guide to the Ownership of Employee Inventions – From Entitlement to Compensation' by James Tumbridge & Ashley Roughton
'A Practical Guide to Asbestos Claims' by Jonathan Owen & Gareth McAloon
'A Practical Guide to Stamp Duty Land Tax in England and Northern Ireland' by Suzanne O'Hara
'A Practical Guide to the Law of Farming Partnerships' by Philip Whitcomb
'Covid-19, Homeworking and the Law – The Essential Guide to Employment and GDPR Issues' by Forbes Solicitors
'Covid-19 and Criminal Law – The Essential Guide' by Ramya Nagesh
'Covid-19 and Family Law in England and Wales – The Essential Guide' by Safda Mahmood

'A Practical Guide to the Law of Unlawful Eviction and Harassment – 2nd Edition' by Stephanie Lovegrove

'Covid-19, Brexit and the Law of Commercial Leases – The Essential Guide' by Mark Shelton

'A Practical Guide to Costs in Personal Injury Claims – 2nd Edition' by Matthew Hoe

'A Practical Guide to the General Data Protection Regulation (GDPR) – 2nd Edition' by Keith Markham

'Ellis on Credit Hire – Sixth Edition' by Aidan Ellis & Tim Kevan

'A Practical Guide to Working with Litigants in Person and McKenzie Friends in Family Cases' by Stuart Barlow

'Protecting Unregistered Brands: A Practical Guide to the Law of Passing Off' by Lorna Brazell

'A Practical Guide to Secondary Liability and Joint Enterprise Post-Jogee' by Joanne Cecil & James Mehigan

'A Practical Guide to the Pre-Action RTA Claims Protocol for Personal Injury Lawyers' by Antonia Ford

'A Practical Guide to Neighbour Disputes and the Law' by Alexander Walsh

'A Practical Guide to Forfeiture of Leases' by Mark Shelton

'A Practical Guide to Coercive Control for Legal Practitioners and Victims' by Rachel Horman

'A Practical Guide to Rights Over Airspace and Subsoil' by Daniel Gatty

'Tackling Disclosure in the Criminal Courts – A Practitioner's Guide' by Narita Bahra QC & Don Ramble

'A Practical Guide to the Law of Driverless Cars – Second Edition' by Alex Glassbrook, Emma Northey & Scarlett Milligan

'A Practical Guide to TOLATA Claims' by Greg Williams

'A Practical Guide to Elderly Law – 2nd Edition' by Justin Patten

'A Practical Guide to Responding to Housing Disrepair and Unfitness Claims' by Iain Wightwick

'A Practical Guide to the Construction and Rectification of Wills and Trust Instruments' by Edward Hewitt

'A Practical Guide to the Law of Bullying and Harassment in the Workplace' by Philip Hyland

'How to Be a Freelance Solicitor: A Practical Guide to the SRA-Regulated Freelance Solicitor Model' by Paul Bennett

'A Practical Guide to Prison Injury Claims' by Malcolm Johnson
'A Practical Guide to the Small Claims Track - 2nd Edition' by Dominic Bright
'A Practical Guide to Advising Clients at the Police Station' by Colin Stephen McKeown-Beaumont
'A Practical Guide to Antisocial Behaviour Injunctions' by Iain Wightwick
'Practical Mediation: A Guide for Mediators, Advocates, Advisers, Lawyers, and Students in Civil, Commercial, Business, Property, Workplace, and Employment Cases' by Jonathan Dingle with John Sephton
'The Mini-Pupillage Workbook' by David Boyle
'A Practical Guide to Crofting Law' by Brian Inkster
'A Practical Guide to Spousal Maintenance' by Liz Cowell
'A Practical Guide to the Law of Domain Names and Cybersquatting' by Andrew Clemson
'A Practical Guide to the Law of Gender Pay Gap Reporting' by Harini Iyengar
'A Practical Guide to the Rights of Grandparents in Children Proceedings' by Stuart Barlow
'NHS Whistleblowing and the Law' by Joseph England
'Employment Law and the Gig Economy' by Nigel Mackay & Annie Powell
'A Practical Guide to Noise Induced Hearing Loss (NIHL) Claims' by Andrew Mckie, Ian Skeate, Gareth McAloon
'An Introduction to Beauty Negligence Claims – A Practical Guide for the Personal Injury Practitioner' by Greg Almond
'Intercompany Agreements for Transfer Pricing Compliance' by Paul Sutton
'Zen and the Art of Mediation' by Martin Plowman
'A Practical Guide to the SRA Principles, Individual and Law Firm Codes of Conduct 2019 – What Every Law Firm Needs to Know' by Paul Bennett
'A Practical Guide to Adoption for Family Lawyers' by Graham Pegg
'A Practical Guide to Industrial Disease Claims' by Andrew Mckie & Ian Skeate
'A Practical Guide to Redundancy' by Philip Hyland
'A Practical Guide to Vicarious Liability' by Mariel Irvine
'A Practical Guide to Applications for Landlord's Consent and Variation of Leases' by Mark Shelton
'A Practical Guide to Relief from Sanctions Post-Mitchell and Denton' by Peter Causton

www.ingramcontent.com/pod-product-compliance
Lightning Source LLC
LaVergne TN
LVHW052256200926
848481LV00002B/385